ONE
GOD

TWO VOICES

PRAISE

"Your message touched my heart repeatedly as I read *One God: Two Voices.* As a retired educator and a Christian, I was so pleased two of my colleagues shared how teachers can spread the love and grace of our Lord inside and outside of the classroom. I know that God wanted to speak to me through new voices, and the two of you provided that opportunity. Your witness to Him is evident from the first word to the last. What an amazing feat. I hope thousands and thousands of teachers read your book and are blessed by your witness and example as I was. It should be on every teacher's reading list. God bless you, my friends."

—Sue Edwards, Retired Principal/Educator

"I was unable to put the book down as it gives a new perspective on educators and the difficult, thankless job they perform day in and day out. Now throw in the fact that both authors are Christian educators with an even higher responsibility! The Two Voices tackle difficult subjects with their individual perspectives, and speak clearly on topics that those in the teacher's lounge and on the street will appreciate because they have discussed, vented, and shrugged their shoulders about them as well. You must own this —it will open your eyes and change your heart!"

—David L. Hancock, Founder Morgan James

"I just wanted to thank you for my very own copy of your book! I started reading it and couldn't put it down. Early Sunday morning, I woke up around 2:00 am and thought I would read a little more until I was ready to go back to sleep. I ended up finishing the entire book by about 5:00 am (need I say more?) I really wondered what I might learn from a book by and for teachers since I am NOT a teacher, but I was intrigued to learn that you two were Christians and didn't mind saying so. Upon actually reading the book, I was proud of how you correlated every chapter with the Gospel. I found it to be very insightful and personally motivating. It is encouraging to know that there are Christians/Teachers like you out there. May God continue to bless the two of you as your 'Voices' reach others."

—Charnita Carmona, Hampton City Schools

ONE
GOD

TWO VOICES

*Life-Changing Lessons From the Classroom
on the Issues Challenging Today's Families*

DEIDRE HESTER
& SUE WHITED

NEW YORK

Published in New York, New York, by Morgan James Publishing. Morgan James and The Entrepreneurial Publisher are trademarks of Morgan James, LLC.
www.MorganJamesPublishing.com

The Morgan James Speakers Group can bring authors to your live event. For more information or to book an event visit The Morgan James Speakers Group at
www.TheMorganJamesSpeakersGroup.com.

Morgan James Publishing
The Entrepreneurial Publisher
5 Penn Plaza, 23rd Floor, New York City, New York 10001
(212) 655-5470 office • (516) 908-4496 fax
www.MorganJamesPublishing.com

A **free** eBook edition is available
with the purchase of this print book.

CLEARLY PRINT YOUR NAME ABOVE IN UPPER CASE
Instructions to claim your free eBook edition:
1. Download the Shelfie app for Android or iOS
2. Write your name in **UPPER CASE** above
3. Use the Shelfie app to submit a photo
4. Download your eBook to any device

9781630477103   paperback
9781630477110   eBook

Library of Congress Control Number:
2015911881

Cover Design by:
Chris Treccani
www.3DogDesign.net

Interior Design by:
Brittany Bondar
www.SageDigitalDesign.com

In an effort to support local communities, raise awareness and funds, Morgan James Publishing donates a percentage of all book sales for the life of each book to
Habitat for Humanity Peninsula and Greater Williamsburg.

Get involved today, visit
www.MorganJamesBuilds.com

Habitat
for Humanity®
Peninsula and
Greater Williamsburg
Building Partner

CONTENTS

PREFACE

An amazing thing happened as Deidre Hester and Sue Whited were concluding their careers as private and public school teachers. They received a call to enter on a mission, carrying a message to all they could reach, both in and out of their teaching professions, about what they had experienced and what they felt God wanted them to share. In 2004, they started the journey to fulfill that mission of being faithful to His calling. Their first endeavor was the creation of the book, *For Such A Time As This . . . We Are But Small Voices*.

During the years that have passed, they have received favorable comments regarding the message that was presented, as well as recommendations to continue their writings. It appeared their mission was not complete. As they began the updating process of their book in 2014, the Lord laid on Deidre's heart that a deeper commitment towards praying and seeking God's will was necessary so their words would be the most effective. With this focus in mind, each began to understand that they were writing from three different identities.

Deidre (Voice I) and Sue (Voice II) are speaking to you through their individual/cultural identities. Not only are they of different races and ages, they were born and raised in different areas and within different kinds of families, which helped to make them the persons they are.

Both of these women have a unique spiritual story which allows them to share from two perspectives. While they were seemingly drawn together and are "sisters in the Lord," they are also God's daughters, and He has shown them different things during their walk with Him.

Probably most alike in their third identity—that of educator—both feel they were gifted by their Creator to teach. It's in their DNA, and they feel entirely alive and invigorated when doing it. Dedicating this work to God because He made it all possible, they also hope to touch a chord in other educators as their voices speak through this combination of the original and updated version of their book. With the support of family and friends, they have continued to answer His call through *One God, Two Voices: Life-Changing Lessons From the Classroom on the Issues Challenging Today's Families*, which adds additional insights and reflections. It is their hope to be a support system for teachers, helping those in the classroom and in the home school to reach out and speak out on topics of interest to them. To that end, they have a website/blog outreach that can connect you to one another. Many voices added to their own have to be a benefit for everyone. Their mission will also include parents and students as they seek to speak and minister to them as well. God bless you as you read—the "voices" hope to hear from you.

"Obedience belongs to us; results belong to God."

www.onegodtwovoices.com

CHAPTER I

The Meeting... and More

"I wish that I could repay a portion of the gladness you've strewn along my way. And if I could have one wish, this only would it be: I'd like to be the kind of friend that you have been to me."
—*Edgar A. Guest*

Voice I:

Who would have ever thought that one person could make such a difference? I mean a difference that would create such an impact that I would never have guessed it would happen to me. Yet it has happened to me and more than once. I believe that God strategically places people in our lives that really make a difference, and I have learned from Maya Angelou to call these individuals that make an impact on us our "lifelines." History has taught us that one person does and can make a difference, either positively or negatively. Consider horrible dictators like Adolf Hitler and Saddam Hussein. It just reminds me to thank the Lord for some of our country's heroes like John F. Kennedy, Martin L. King, Jr., and the main hero who belongs to me as well as millions of other Christians, Jesus Christ, our Lord and Savior. But for me, Sue is one of my favorite and personal heroes who entered my life in the fall of 1990, and this walk of mine has never been the same.

Sue Whited was the name she stated when we met, and I was impressed by her full, gorgeous set of brown, wavy hair. I remember her being taller than the average female and middle aged. Upon further observation, I saw her put so much excitement and great exuberance into the current task at hand that I easily guessed that she loved teaching.

I, on the other hand, loved the students and was still trying to acquire a love for teaching, which was not my first choice of careers. "Now she looks like a real teacher," I remember thinking as well. Not that I didn't feel like a real teacher because I felt I could teach. I just did not want to teach and had to learn the hard way that teaching, like preaching, is ordained by God (Ephesians 4:11). At that time, teaching jobs were the only doors God would open for me because He was specifically showing me how to submit to His will. I don't know how I looked, but Sue just had that teacher's look and I noticed it the very first day we met. You might see her in the grocery store and correctly guess, "That's a teacher." Even one of our former students called me over to his desk one day to show me a picture in a magazine. "Mrs. Hester," he stated, "Doesn't that look like Mrs. Whited with that sign—looking like a teacher-teacher?" Professional decorum disappeared as I fell out laughing while my other students looked on as if I had gone mad. That day "teacher-teacher," a term coined by our former student, was incorporated into my vocabulary. A teacher-teacher:

> Stands up 95% of the time while teaching.
> Arrives early to prepare for the day.
> Stays late at work to plan for tomorrow.
> Takes work home and actually does it.
> Makes detailed lesson plans and grades every project.
> Checks to make sure homework is completed.
> Spends his/her own money on the students and classroom supplies.
> Makes phone calls home to let parents know about problems before it's too late.
> Sponsors several activities and/or clubs for the students.
> Would rather come in sick than have a "sub" fill in for the day.

Has enough sick and personal days on the books to retire a
few years early.

Is selected Teacher of the Year every year by someone (including a relative or friend).

We have all probably known at least one teacher who fits that description, but Sue is definitely one that I know personally. I have often said
to her, "I wish I had had you as a teacher in the eighth grade, and I
pray each year for my children to have a teacher like you." The great
thing about that is how God has done exactly that more than once.

Sue's initial approach towards me was warm, friendly, and full of life.
I liked her instantly, and after that one encounter, I felt myself drawn
to her like a moth to a light. This tall, amicable woman appealed to
me as sensitive, experienced, and wise. Somehow I just knew that I
would learn from her, drawing from her like a really dry sponge
absorbing water. Each day we found ourselves engaged in one-on-one
conversations.

I have Sue to thank for my voting in each election. I had shared with
her on one of those rare occasions when you take a risk with someone
you're getting to know and say something deep, straight from the
heart. You take this risk with that person and hope they will still like
you and consider you an equal after you have said it. Sue taught social
studies on our team, so the topic of current events came up often as
we talked. Election time was quickly approaching, and Sue wanted to
have some type of mock election with our classes (I say "our" classes
because in middle school a team of two to four teachers teaches the
same group of students in order to plan and correlate lessons/sub-
jects). Needless to say, what two better subjects could you have to
work together than language arts, my subject, and social studies? As
Sue began to animatedly go over her plans for a mock election during

our team planning time, she looked for me to grasp the excitement and tell her what English skills could best be tied into the lesson. As I sat and watched Sue, it was obvious that I was much less enthused than she. "So what do you think?" she asked. Take the risk, I thought, and suddenly my reply just gushed out of me like a child harboring a deep, dark secret. "How am I going to get our students involved in a process I haven't even participated in yet myself?" Sue looked at me, but not down at me, so from that point I let it all out. I shared with her how as a young black woman, I felt the system was full of mainly white males who held the top positions, with top pay, and we probably would never have a black president because of who I called "the powers that be." I went on to ask, "Why should I vote? I am a nobody in a white man's world." I was bitter indeed, but I sensed Sue's compassionate ear close by as I shared even more and ended with my confession that I had never voted.

By the time Sue finished with me that day, I felt proud to be an American and was ready to vote. As I made plans to register for my first election, I became excited and easily began to think of ways English would tie in perfectly with a mock election. Amazingly, as I look back, it wasn't the gruesome details of dog bites, beatings, or any lynching that caused me to go to the polls. The knowledge of struggles blacks had faced during the Civil Rights movement with the loss of many loved ones and heroes, known and unknown, was still not enough to make me vote. How ironic it was that my good friend, a white woman, had been the most influential in my decision to exercise my 15th Amendment rights. Some people would say that I should be ashamed of being an educator and not voting, but I say it was issues that had stood in the way. God provided a way out for me. Sue was sent into my life for specific reasons, and that was just one of them. Today she is one of the closest friends I have.

On the surface one might be amazed at how our friendship may appear to break some obvious social rules. She is fifteen years my senior and a southern Baptist from a small town in West Virginia. I, on the other hand, am nondenominational (many would say Pentecostal "holy roller"), and a native of Brooklyn, New York. Sometimes I think of myself as a Brooklyn chick because I was born and spent much of my formative years there before my family and I moved to a very small, rural area in North Carolina called Gates County. Somehow we found each other, and when we taught together, we made an awesome team that made a positive impact on those we taught and knew, both professionally and personally. This is our story about how we believe God has brought us together for our own personal growth and development, but most importantly, for others. It is our hope that by sharing our story, others can learn and be healed in some small way, either professionally or personally. We hope the Light that lives within us will be glorified because we have come to realize that even though we are no longer working together, we are still on the same team, with the same goals that will allow our lives to bring glory to Him.

Voice II:

In 1990 I was beginning my third year as a middle school social studies teacher, and was in the midst of moving to my third classroom in as many years. It was hot and the air conditioning was not on yet in the classrooms. As my fan whirled loudly, I found myself surrounded by stacks of posters, boxes of books, masking tape, and markers that fourth week of August. Up on a ladder to put yet another poster in just the right place, I heard a voice asking if I knew where a certain room was located. I looked down and there was an attractive, young, black teacher pushing an umbrella stroller with a little girl in it. She introduced herself, and I learned that this was Deidre Hester, my eighth grade team's new language arts teacher. My first impression was: good, we need a black teacher on our team; my second, what a beautiful smile.

Deidre and I seemed to bond almost immediately. She soon became as busy as I was trying to get her room ready. When the four teachers on our team met, she and I seemed to agree as to what we wanted for our students. I was more than willing to help her fit into the school routine and answer any questions she might have. Day after day, we always were together—talking either before or after school, or both. At first glance, we seemed to be an unlikely pair. She was much younger with a year-old daughter, and I was much older, with both of my sons in their twenties. I was raised in West Virginia, and she came from New York City by way of rural North Carolina. Despite our many differences, we soon discovered our most important similarity—we were both Christians. It seemed that our hearts drew us together in a friendship that would overcome race, age, and background. It wasn't an immediate process, but happened over a period of weeks, months, and years. The most important thing was that it happened.

My experiences with Deidre, both personally and professionally, have impacted my life in a wonderful way. I took a leap of faith in attending church services with her occasionally, and experienced the joy of her church's worship style which was very different from my own. I traveled to North Carolina and met her extended family, enjoying some of the best country cooking I've ever eaten. I even asked my husband, Richard, to help with the remodeling of Deidre's and her husband, Larry's, home. But most importantly, I was honored to be there when their son, Larry Donnell Hester, Jr., was born. Adding to that joy was the fact that Richard and I became Larry J's Godparents. Deidre made me a better teacher because what I learned from my friendship with her made me a more knowledgeable and accepting person and was multiplied into many more lives. She became a part of many memorable classroom experiences, helping to inspire our students to achieve. God placed us together for a reason, and even though we no longer work together, we are still working for Him through our sharing, praying, laughter, and tears. What we have together is too good to keep to ourselves, so we are sharing it with you, our readers.

TWO VOICES AS ONE

Are you a risk-taker in life? Have you ever taken a chance and gotten to know someone who is very different from you? Throughout our five years of teaching together, we tried to show our students that "you can't judge a book by its cover," and encouraged them to share their lives with as many different types of people as they could. Not only did we teach this concept, we modeled it. It was our hope that they would be as blessed as we have been. Now we are taking our story and experiences to another audience—our readers. We hope for the same results as we did with our students. We challenge you to reach beyond your comfort zone and become a risk-taker. God may bless you as He has us, and your life will never be the same.

TEN YEARS LATER

Deidre's Voice:

"WOW! Ten years later." As I look back over our "voices," an immediate desire to present a couple of rebuttals is now a matter of necessity. The first regarding, "it reminds me to thank the Lord for heroes like J. F. Kennedy and M. L. King (pg. 2 Voice I, 1st ed.)" After ten years of a variety of documentaries, books, and movies on the lives of these two men, there is no doubt in the minds of many that JFK was a charismatic womanizer and MLK, Jr. could have had a similar problem according to the FBI. Yet, both still remain a hero to many, including me. This is mainly because they helped further the Civil Rights Movement in several powerful ways including the loss of their lives. My other comment, was about a black man never becoming President. Well, I have to thoroughly eat those words although it was really hard for me to vote for President Obama for a second term when he openly endorsed same-sex "marriage" because I believe that marriage is God-ordained and therefore God-defined. Honestly, I did not want to vote for Obama at all, but my strong religious belief system would not allow me to vote for a known Mormon. I almost felt like I did ten or more years ago—no need to vote. Expect more on that subject in our recap of "We Agree to Disagree" (Lol—now also a relative term ten years later). I must add with some conviction though that I felt really proud when President Obama won his first election. To see black faces like mine standing out on that arena in Chicago was a feeling I will never forget. I shared this emotional connection with millions, including Oprah Winfrey, as I watched the tears streaming down her face. I think President Obama, First Lady Michelle and their daughters look really good together as a family. They have that special charismatic look to them, which reminds me of pictures that I have seen of the Kennedy family.

To date, both Sue and Richard are still a huge part of our lives as they were right there when my husband recently retired from 25 years of service in the U.S. Navy. During a special part of his ceremony, I heard my husband state how we would not be where we are without them, as they taught us a lot about living and enjoying life. I smiled and nodded easily in agreement as I thought about a variety of events we had been fortunate enough to share. The Godson Sue witnessed the birth of nineteen years ago is now in college. Of course Sue and Richard were right there with us as we made that first sorrowful deposit of our youngest child which proved to be more painful for me than my husband, as I cried enough tears for us both. The darling daughter Sue can still picture from over twenty years ago sitting in that umbrella stroller now has a darling daughter of her own. Saniyah Grace is our first and only grandchild and an absolute Godsend.

You may have correctly assumed how Sue was right there to encourage me through it all as we became the novice "empty-nesters" just as they had reached the delightful, joyful, and pro-status of the highly experienced empty nest team. Indeed, we have continued to laugh, cry, and trust God together even though we spend more time apart from one another further distanced by our new Florida residence once we left Japan. Yet modern technology keeps our hearts and minds connected which further cements how Sue is my sister for life.

Sue's Voice:

All of us have our individual pathways through life. Most contain the same progression: family, school, friends, interests, education, jobs, marriage, children, retirement, and decline. It's interesting to look back, to self-assess after a period of time, events from our lives, and that is what I'm doing now with our *Small Voices* book. My pathway has led to retirement from the classroom, but definitely not from life. In the ten years since the publishing of our book, my husband and I have built our retirement home in the "Whited Woods" of WV, cared for dying parents, become active in our local church, traveled to the mountains and the seashores, visited with our son as often as possible back in Virginia, and enjoyed camping experiences. When I pick up the book and reread Ch. 1, I can still see Deidre and her darling daughter, Shamona, as I described them in that chapter. I continue to be amazed at how our friendship developed, but I can see God's hand in it all. He brought us together to share life's experiences and be a support system for one another. I have prayed for her family and children as she has prayed for mine. A lot has happened on both sides that we never expected and for which we couldn't prepare. Having a close friend on which we could rely, despite the miles of separation, made all the difference for both of us. We have had joyful times as well, enjoying scenery, music, and fun as we have visited and vacationed together. Through it all, nothing has changed—time stands still when we are together; it's as though we haven't been apart. She is my forever friend and a valued voice in my life. I'm so glad I opened myself up to the possibility of an unlikely friendship.

"Good friends are like stars. You don't always see them but you know they are there."
—Christy Evans

CHAPTER II

Teacher to Teacher: Why Teach?

"If you have knowledge, let others light their candles at it."
—*Margaret Fuller*

Voice I:

"I don't want to teach nobody's 'bad a** kids!" This was what I was thinking when my college English professor suggested that I take education courses since I had already completed my English requirements at the end of my junior year in college. Instead I somehow managed to get out one audible phrase, "If you think so; you're my advisor, so I guess I should." Looking back, I thank God that He delivered me from such filthy language and provided the means for my grammar to improve.

I had come to Livingstone College by chance, or so I thought at the time, in order to receive my BA in English, and then transfer on to a major university to get a degree in Speech Pathology and Audiology. A doctor by the name of Gaither at Hampton General Hospital was responsible for fostering that desire within me. I had read an article about how he gave people a new lease on life when he would rehabilitate them from near-death experiences after being in car crashes. They would have to have reconstructive surgery and therapy to re-teach them childhood speech and language skills. From that point on, I knew that was what I wanted to do in some form or another. Prior to this, I had really planned to pursue a career in acting after undergraduate school, but now this seemed like a more realistic goal. I reminded my advisor that my BA in English would just be a stepping stone to a far greater calling than teaching ever would be. She reminded me that teaching would provide some well—needed funds for graduate school, as well as be something I could "fall back on." With that said, I registered for education requirements, and have been "falling back" on teaching ever since. Really in retrospect, I don't think my distaste for teaching bad kids was the real reason I wanted to avoid teaching. In reality, I just didn't feel competent enough to teach a pet, much less someone else's child. That is why I feel so strongly that teaching was God's plan for my life. Even with so many odds stacked against me, I became the first person in my family to graduate from college, and I did so "Cum Laude."

I grew up the sixth of eight children in a family whose lives would be torn apart by the separation of a marriage and the death of my father. The result of these experiences left me receiving my formative training at Deauville Gardens Elementary in Long Island, N.Y., PS 73 in Brooklyn, N.Y., PS 128 in Queens, N.Y., and Gatesville Elementary in Gates County, N.C. These childhood educational experiences left me feeling inadequate, particularly when I moved from Amityville, N.Y., to Brooklyn, then Queens, and then a drastic change to schools in the South. Standardized tests I had taken in New York dictated that my placement should be in the above average classes. Unfortunately, when entering PS 73, the principal informed my mother that there were no "B-slot" classes available, so she could choose to put me in the "A-class" or the "D-class." Unaware of the detriment this would later cause me when we moved to N.C., my mother allowed me to choose for myself. Looking into the "A-Class," I saw lots of hard work, lists of assignments on the board, and students engrossed in books and papers. As I looked into the "D-Class," I saw students working puzzles, playing games, and having fun. Is it any wonder that I chose the "D-Class?"

This choice had a long-term effect on my educational skills, but some-how the hand of God even turned that to my good because it was in the "D-Class" that I met Mr. Levine. He threw me my first lifeline by encouraging, challenging, and exposing not only me, but also a few others in my class of inner-city children to the life beyond the drug infested, crime-ridden brutal streets of Brooklyn, NY. Somehow Mr. Levine must have known intuitively that we were not meant to be in the "D-Class!" This Sonny Bono look-alike took us to New York University as a part of a class project when he was working on his Master's degree, and exposed us to the life of higher learning. He took us out to eat, on walks through the college campus and the park, and fed us Drake's "devil dogs," which are chocolate cakes filled with whipped cream and shaped like a hot dog. We devoured those delicious treats while discussing our futures. He also built up our self-esteem by allowing us to perform in plays which he wrote. Of course, I always had a leading role! I remember one play in particular, entitled *Pollution is a Crime*. It featured a song to the tune of "Love Potion #9." I played a character called Smoggy Sam, who thought it profitable to pollute the air with aerosol spray cans. This was my acting debut, and my mother, oldest brother, and uncle were all there. They told me how I was a star performer, and I believed that until high school. That was the first experience to foster my thoughts into believing my future would involve acting. Yet it was this teacher, Mr. Levine, whose loving nature and caring ways helped me remember years later, how just one teacher made all the difference in my life.

I never thought I could be a "Mr. Levine." Yet God's plan would prevail as I was offered a teaching job just two weeks prior to graduating. The Mecklenburg County School system in Charlotte, N.C., gave me a contract teaching seventh through ninth grade English classes, contingent on my passing the National Teaching Exam. I did pass and accepted it as the miracle I needed to begin my teaching career. These events allowed me to begin to understand how God really does make the impossibilities of our lives a reality when we do our part.

When I began teaching, I wanted out right after my very first summer of teaching summer school to inner-city youth in Charlotte, N.C. I literally tried to get as far away from teaching as I could, but my experience would always lead me right back to the front door of the classroom. One day I shared this reoccurring urge to leave the teaching profession with my pastor who is another lifeline of mine. He encouraged me strongly to stay in the teaching field. He said that I should ride out those difficult moments and never quit because God needs His people everywhere, especially in the public school system. It was in 1988 that he said, "One day teachers will receive the pay and respect they deserve." So again, as I had back in college, I took the advice from a person solely based upon who he was in society and who he was to me. I would come to fully realize what Bishop Boone, my foundation pastor and oldest brother, meant. It is God who instills the gift of teaching (Ephesians 4:11—"It was He who gave some to be . . . teachers"). Teachers have that gift and are gifts to everyone who has ever received some form of education for any time period or for any reason in their life. I may not have always felt fully competent enough in the academic arena of language arts, but God had chosen me! His choice was enough to give me the motivation to study, work, and practice hard in my content area, and my skills did improve immensely. I discovered I could teach because "I can do all things through Christ who strengthens me." (Philippians 4:13)

"With God all things are possible"—Matthew 19:26

Voice II:

I came to the teaching profession later than most, but I truly believe that I was born to teach. I always enjoyed school as a child. Reading was and continues to be a joy, but math and science required a lot of work on my part. Nevertheless, I always did well in school because I knew that I was expected to do my best, and my best was A's and B's. Placed in high academic-tracked classes—they were called accelerated in my day—I made a U-turn my senior year of high school and decided that I wanted to work after graduation. Whether it was the tumultuous campuses of the mid 1960s or the serious relationship I had with my long-term boyfriend, Richard, I decided that college wasn't for me and changed my math and science classes for business courses. After graduation, I worked in the business sector until my marriage at the very young age of "almost nineteen."

The long-term boyfriend, now my husband, was an airman in the U. S. Air Force, and in 1967 we began a 20-year tour of duty at various bases throughout the Midwest and Southeastern United States. Two sons, Ric and Bryan, were born to us, and I thoroughly enjoyed being a mother to two very bright boys. From the beginning, I would talk to my babies, teaching them about colors, numbers, and the names of everything we encountered. They were my first students, and I remember ordering books for them when we really couldn't afford them, believing that books held the key for their futures. I volunteered with the Boy Scouts and became a part-time Sunday school and Bible school teacher, and did the normal "mother" things, like baking cupcakes for school birthday parties and working booths for school carnivals. Whenever I worked in the school setting, I noticed that I really felt invigorated and energized. I enjoyed being there as much as I used to when I was a student, but didn't realize that this was the setting where I should be working until several years later.

After attending junior college part-time in Mississippi and Florida, the boys and I moved home to West Virginia while the military man of our family completed a remote tour of duty in South Korea. Once again I tried the business world, working in a job placement agency. I rationalized that it would take a lot of time and money to complete a college degree in education and decided that I should concentrate on secretarial work, enjoying my family and volunteer activities instead. This mind-set worked for the remainder of the year of separation.

When my husband returned, he was assigned to Langley AFB in Hampton, Virginia, and within two months of our relocating to this area, I had become a secretary employed in of all places, a school. The first time I walked into Syms Junior High School, it felt right; it even smelled right! I loved the work—it was fast-paced and the teachers, counselors, and administrators were real professionals and fun people with whom to work. After a year or so there, during which I got used to working with students in grades seven through nine, I mentioned to several of the guidance counselors that I thought I would enjoy teaching. They were so supportive that I inquired about evening classes at the local Christopher Newport College (now University). The next five to six years were the most exciting, but exhausting years I had ever experienced in my life. Looking back, I give God the credit for seeing me through such a challenging time. I worked full-time at Syms, which by now had become a middle school with sixth through eighth grade students, and attended classes part-time. I continued to be a wife and mom, keeping the house cleaned, the laundry done, the groceries bought, the suppers cooked, and the dogs fed. I know, I should have expected my family to take up the slack, but I was determined that they would not pay for my starting late to complete the degree that I now realized I should have obtained years earlier. I was relentless in my expectations of my college work, using every spare minute to study and prepare. Even the bathroom became a study room, as I would pore over notes in the bathtub and recite speeches in front of the mirror as I curled my hair.

All the hard work paid off in May, 1988, when I graduated Summa Cum Laude with a degree in Elementary Education and a concentration in, I believe, the most difficult area to teach, middle school. I graduated already hired—I would teach, not the sixth graders I had requested, but remedial eighth graders—the big guys and gals, most of whom had already failed at least once. I would need my prayers now more than ever! The first year of teaching taught me more than I had ever learned in college about teaching methods, classroom management, parent/teacher communication, and how important my underlying reasons for becoming a teacher really were.

I became a teacher to make a difference in the lives of my students. I have always believed that the subject matter is important, but that my students also need to know about life, values, and the consequences of their choices as well. Before the advent of Virginia's SOLs (Standards of Learning), I had more time to dwell on these important "extras," but I still found time to work them into my lessons or the curriculum because, sadly, some of my students would not be exposed to them anywhere else. I became "Mama Whited" to a vast majority of my students and enjoyed the interaction of studies and life that happened in my classroom every day.

When Deidre came on my teaching team, she completed what I started with our students, and I did the same for her. We were on the same page, drawing from the same strengths as we held the line on behavior, completion of assignments, and classroom expectations. We were the "dynamic duo" of Team 8C!

TWO VOICES AS ONE…FOR YOU

The teaching profession is an honorable one that affects many lives. Ask anyone you know, and they will remember a particular teacher who changed their life, either for better or worse. The way the teacher spoke, favorite phrases, a particular memorable incident in that class, etc. These memories will go on forever. We believe the most effective teachers are not made; they are born ("We have different gifts . . . if it is teaching, let him teach," Rom. 12:6-7). We were fortunate that our teaching philosophies meshed, since we both feel that all children can learn. However, we also understand that this learning takes place in different ways and through different methods. This makes the job of an educator very difficult at times. However, when the "light bulb" comes on in your students' eyes, and you know that understanding has taken place, the effort is worth it. Doing whatever it takes for the necessary results requires a special teacher who is willing to invest time, talent, and creativity in lesson plans. Being a misplaced actor doesn't hurt either, as Deidre and I both discovered at times!

Teachers, don't worry that you are not working for a Fortune 500 company or earning a higher paycheck. Don't listen to the naysayers who continually criticize the public education system because they aren't talking about you. If you believe that you were born to teach, hang in there! At the end of the day and the school year, you can look back and realize that you were involved in the second most influential career in the world. After parenthood, teachers personally affect the future in powerful ways. You may be the only positive light in a child's life, so don't take your position lightly.

TEN YEARS LATER

Deidre's Voice:

Ten years have gone by, and I still see a great need for the teacher's voice to be heard and respected on a larger level. This is because many decisions are still being made from the "Ivory Towers" (administration, law-makers), and so many of them have nothing to do with the reality of actually being in the trenches that teachers are still digging out of on a daily basis. These trenches include more emphasis on standards of learning and barrier tests that students must pass before they can be promoted to the next grade level. Each state sets these standards based on President Bush's "No Child Left Behind" Act of 2001. These rigorous standards place more emphasis on the teacher to perform and get *IT* accomplished at any cost. *IT*—the test information, skills and strategies—has to be taught or the teachers may not receive merit pay or could be penalized with low evaluation reports. In many cases the teacher cannot enjoy teaching his or her subject of choice anymore. In my opinion, this has become one of the largest travesties in our educational system.

I once communicated to one of our former presidents stating how I feel that one of the biggest problems we face today in our schools is the lack of equal technology at every public and private school. I believe the disparity in this area is huge because many schools with limited financing can only provide the basics, while other schools are able to provide the latest and best of everything. We cannot expect one teacher in a classroom of 20 to 30 students to meet every need each day without proper assistance and support. Adequate computer labs, individual laptop computers for more students, WiFi access throughout buildings, Smart white boards or just adequate electrical wiring that will allow technology to exist in more classrooms are needed necessities. Students tend to learn how they live which today is through vivid color, high definition sound, and hands-on virtual reality experiences. Learning methods have advanced and the infrastructure of our schools needs help to keep up with them. The latest technology being made available to every U.S. student in each classroom would be a great equalizer.

Additionally, this is not the 20th century with one teacher teaching first grade through twelfth, although for many teachers, that is what it resembles, when you consider that many students are now being main-streamed. Therefore, one teacher could have several students diagnosed with ADD, ADHD, autism, hearing impairment or an array of learning disabilities with each having an Individual Assessment Plan that must be followed (by law), all in one class. A typical classroom now looks like a three-ring circus as the teacher/ringmaster has to accommodate his/her daily lessons to meet many individual needs. In addition, teacher aides that come into the classroom to assist special-needs students also need to have a copy of the lesson plans with the appropriate adjustments on it already in place for the aide to follow. More and more continues to be added to the teacher's plate with no additional time to accommodate these additional responsibilities.

When you consider that so many adjustments are being made for students and parents as well, such as home-schooled students, virtual classes, after school alternative classes, dual enrollment classes, Advanced Placement classes, International Baccalaureate (IB) programs and the like, it is no wonder that teacher burnout happens so often. I suggest that the "powers that be" get with the "powers who are" and begin to have some honest dialogue on what needs to be done to help our teachers assist with improving and revamping the educational system in America. The fact that we are considered one of the world's most powerful nations, but our students consistently rank as average as or even lower than many countries is totally alarming. In 2012, the Program for International Student Assessment testing of 15-year olds ranked the United States as slightly below average among 65 nations in math, science, and reading.* After living in Japan for three years and witnessing their school culture and their students' work ethic, I would have to acknowledge that our country is lacking. Of course you have arguments on both sides, but many educators know how far behind our students are academically. Ironically, having more material things and resources available to them is also why so many of our American students lack creativity, productivity, accountability and stability. I have to strongly agree with Sue's husband, Richard, when he remarked that learning used to be done for learning's sake. There is nothing inherently <u>fun</u> about math, science, reading, or foreign languages, but today's classrooms are given the impossible task of making these subjects fun and engaging, or the students lose interest and don't learn. In addition, I believe an increase in cultural diversity is also a factor in our lower international rankings. Many schools now have to include English as a second language (ESE) classes in order to accommodate the huge increase of children of immigrants, legal and illegal, who now attend many of our schools, with the classroom teacher bearing the brunt of the responsibility.

Sadly, our American schools have also chosen to leave God out of the equation, for which we are paying a huge price that increases with each passing school year. Our educational system was founded on Godly principles and standards, but we have removed this most important foundation. And now, we are slowly deteriorating like an infested sore on a gangrened foot. We are increasingly rotting away while many of our spoiled children are allowed to have ten pairs of Jordan/Nike shoes, a TV, computer, I-phone, X-Box or the like in their bedroom with little to no supervision; all while bringing home D's and F's on their report card. What have they done to earn all these special things? Meanwhile in the classroom, the teacher has to try to compete with all of this new technology, sometimes with little-to-no effect. Unfortunately, the adolescent mind is also contending with modern technology, becoming saturated with vivid sexual and violent images offered by U-Tube, Google, and video games. Is it any wonder that our test scores are down?

Many of our young people do not even respect their parents, so they in turn will not respect the teacher or other authority figures. "Pants on the ground" and full-bodied tattoos are replacing the youth's image and desire to be like mom and dad. Too often these parents are out of place as well, with many now divorced two or three times, "shacking up" with boyfriends or girlfriends, or living and teaching homosexual lifestyles as the new norm for our family structure. It has all become a vicious cycle of who is to blame for the downward spiral of our students. Regardless of blame, the end result is the same and totally unacceptable, and reminds me of what President Ronald Reagan once said: "We are never defeated unless we give up on God."

I say, "hats-off" to all teachers remaining in the public schools. Be the light and the salt because it is well-needed. I remained with public school education for a little over fourteen years and grew tremendously as a person. Ten years later, God has moved me to the Christian education arena because He wants me to be the Mary McLeod Bethune of Christian education in order to boldly proclaim His works, His word, and His goodness everyday and all throughout the day, as much as possible. As the MMB of Christian education, I have a right to pray, carry my Bible, read my Bible, or say, "Praise God" openly. I want to candidly display His goodness, love and mercy at Christmas (not winter break), Easter (not Spring break) and Valentine's Day (because God is Love!). I am getting too old to tone it down or walk on egg shells because I do not want to offend others with my "fanatical" belief in God. As a Christian, I have rights too! I want everyone to know that the best education must uphold God and His standards.

"Why teach?" That's so easily acceptable to me now because I fully embrace and understand that I was born to preach, teach, and encourage in whatever order it becomes necessary. God revealed to me that there are **generations** of children coming up who have no knowledge of who He really is and His desire to be a part of their everyday lives. Every child needs to know he or she was put on this earth for a specific reason, and we need to freely seek our Creator for our best use and function. We all have an obvious design and purpose; this design implies a designer! ** His name is Jesus. (John 1:15). To this I simply reply, "Here I am! Send me!" Oh . . . and can someone help me find Mr. Levine?

> "If we don't teach our children to follow Christ,
> the world will teach them not to."
> —Unknown

*Carol L. Mitchell, Parkersburg (WV) News & Sentinel Letters to the Editor, (4/27/14)
**Credit: Intelligent Design Movement

Sue's Voice:

Even after retirement, I still feel an affinity with teachers. I can't drive by a school without wondering what is going on inside those classrooms. Parents' open house announcements on the reader boards bring back memories of those long days, and holiday programs remind me of past student performances. I hear news about a lockdown at a nearby school or a tragedy in a far-away state, and my mind is right there with all those involved.

In remembering that first year or two of teaching, I wonder how I ever made it through. The Assistant Superintendent of Schools for the city of Hampton visited my classroom on my VERY FIRST DAY OF TEACHING! That first day is crazy anyway, and I had to be more nervous than the eighth graders who walked through the door—and there he was. Thankfully, he was a gem of a man, smiled throughout his visit, and left me a note of encouragement that I kept for years.

Within the first six weeks of teaching, I, along with all the other new teachers, was evaluated through the BTAP system (Beginning Teacher's Assistance Program). That's all I needed—a seasoned veteran sitting in the back of my room, scrutinizing my lesson plan and marking whether or not I fulfilled the ten necessary benchmarks for my profession. Remember, I was teaching the remedial eighth graders—no problem there with behavioral issues! It's a wonder that I lasted one year, yet alone almost two decades in the classroom.

Some teachers don't last more than one year because the problem of teacher retention has continued to plague the profession. While research shows that the Baby Boomer generation retirees are a factor in the turnover rates, almost twice as many who leave are new teachers who cite stress, job dissatisfaction, and the need to find a new career as reasons for leaving the classroom. The National Commission on Teaching and America's Future estimates that one-third of all new teachers leave teaching after three years, and up to fifty percent are gone within five years. This "revolving door" of teacher loss is costing roughly $7 billion yearly as school districts attempt to recruit, hire, and retrain new teachers. What a loss, both financially and professionally. Of course, teaching is not a good match for some people, and their loss is probably for the best. However others might just need time and mentoring by those who understand both the profession and the students. Some school districts are actively promoting this concept by pairing up new teachers with veterans on the staff. With support, some new teachers might decide to remain longer and help to increase the retention rate.

I recently read an article by Sarah Blaine from her *parentingthecore* blog concerning her experience with the teaching profession. She left after two years, earned a law degree, and discovered that she could expect to make about five times as much in this new profession than she did in her previous one. Here's an excerpt:

"We all know what teachers do, right? After all, we were all students. Each one of us sat through class after class for thirteen years, and encountered dozens of teachers. So we know teachers. We get teachers. We know which teachers are effective, we know which ones left lasting impressions, we know which teachers changed our lives, and we know which ones sucked. We know which teachers changed lives for the better. We know which ones changed lives for the worse. **We are wrong.** We need to honor teachers. We need to respect teachers. We need to listen to teachers. We need to stop reducing teachers to arbitrary measurements of student growth on so-called objective exams. Most of all, we need to stop thinking that we know anything about teaching merely by virtue of having once been students. **We don't know.** The problem with teaching as a profession is that every single adult citizen of this country thinks that they know what teachers do. So they prescribe solutions, and they develop public policy, and they editorialize, and they politicize. And they don't listen to those who do know. Those who can teach. **The teachers.**"

I think Ms. Blaine and Deidre are on the same page, don't you? Those who know the profession are rarely asked for reality-based solutions to the problems teachers face. Those new to teaching are expected to come in from day one and produce results in what can be very difficult circumstances. Speaking from my time in the classroom, I found that experience was the best teacher. My husband had said as much to me as I approached my second year of teaching. He had begun his career as a high school math teacher after retiring from the Air Force, and told me that my second year as a teacher would be much easier. He was absolutely right, and I truly developed my own personal style that year and felt much more comfortable as an educator. That must have been what Deidre observed upon meeting me, as that happened at the start of my third year of teaching. I was able to use my experiences in the classroom as well as in life to help her feel comfortable on our team. God's timing was perfect as usual.

I totally agree with Deidre in wondering what the future holds for American education. Right now **IT'S NOT WORKING** for the majority of students! It seems the school boards and administrations across our country continue to try the latest fads in education, but there is little long-term improvement. Why not return to something that worked for generations? Somehow we must enlighten the parents and students to the importance of working now for results later. Missing school for shopping trips, mini-vacations, doctor's appointments that turn into eating out and missing the entire day—these are not the child's fault, but they impact their education tremendously. What absent students miss is important, and instruction is never the same when it's a makeup assignment. Leaving God out, but bringing the modern culture in has not been good for our children either. The evidence is clear—we continue to slip in the education polls and that matters. Where will we be in another generation?

Deidre and I have developed a blog for our profession, where we can expound on topics and listen to your responses. Once this re-do of our book is completed, that is the next step. I hope we can count on you, the current professionals who are actively trudging through the trenches of public, private, and home schools to participate.* We need and want to learn from you and those who have left the profession for retirement, other careers, or parenthood.

Ok, it's time to turn the page as we're about to write about your clients and their parents!

*www.onegodtwovoices.com

CHAPTER III

Teacher to Parent

*"Children learn best from example; the trouble is, they
don't know a good example from a bad one."*
—*Anonymous*

Voice I:

My desire in this chapter is to send a message to all parents, but in particular, I feel the need to reach out to the black moms in society. So first, I simply say to all parents: "Please stop spoiling your child beyond repair because once you begin to defend your child whether he/she is right or wrong or even before you have all the facts, you reinforce the idea that your child does not have to accept full responsibility for his/her own actions."

From a black woman's perspective, I have witnessed first-hand, time and time again mothers of my black students coming to their aid with feathers all ruffled and with a "full-cocked barrel," ready to verbally shoot anyone putting the blame on their precious children. I believe they go into battle for them because from a black perspective, history has demonstrated that society has damaged our people, especially our men. By acting this way, they're saying, "I refuse to be a partaker in also damaging the black male's ego, dignity, and self-respect." They want to shield their sons from the degradation and the shame that has been passed down from generation to generation to our boys from society as a whole. The only problem with this is that our boys become men—men who have not learned that wrong choices have negative consequences, and that mom will not or cannot always be there to defend them.

We need our men to be involved in the lives of our sons. Women can't always successfully rear and train boys, so thank God for the male teachers in our elementary and middle schools. No matter how much a mother wants to raise her son, in reality, it takes a man to make a man and show him by example. I could never teach my son to be a man because I'm not a man. Unfortunately, many single moms don't have an available male to be a positive influence and role model in the lives of their children. In these situations, I would suggest outside activities like scouting, the YMCA, mentoring organizations like Big Brother, and church youth activities where male leadership can help.

My message to all parents is to stop making excuses for your sons and daughters. Make them responsible for every action and hold your child accountable. Take the time from your job and visit their schools. Communicate with their teachers consistently and get to know them. If the teacher tells you they are misbehaving, they probably are. If your student isn't doing his/her work, find out why and become part of the solution, not part of the problem. When you work with the teacher and not against him or her, everyone wins, especially your child.

> "Kids don't need another friend. What they need
> is a parent to be a parent."
> —Judge Judy Sheindlin

Voice II:

Part of a teacher's job is interacting not only with students, but also with their parents. For some, this is a learned skill; for others, it remains very difficult for a variety of reasons. Moms and dads, single moms or dads, grandparents, and other relatives don't want to hear that "your child is not doing his or her work," "your child is not behaving in class," or "your child is not accepting responsibility." Somehow this is a reflection on them. Some of the most difficult parts of teaching can involve the adults in your students' lives. If I could speak to the world of parents out there, this is what I would say: "Parents, please allow me to teach your children and hold them accountable for their work and actions. Stop making excuses for them when there are no acceptable excuses."

Children learn early how to play parent against parent, and once in school, parent against teacher. When that inevitable note or phone call comes, the child is ready with many reasons why the teacher is unfair, prejudiced, or just plain mean. Speaking for myself and many other teachers, I would say that we simply don't have the time to pick on your child. We are too busy trying to teach from one to six classes per day, depending on the grade level. Am I always totally fair? Maybe I'm not, because I am human and can make mistakes. When I do, I try to model the right behavior and apologize to the child in front of the class. How can I expect them to show respect, if I don't lead the way?

Many students have started down the road to ruin because the adults in their lives don't hold them accountable to a high standard of work and behavior. They fight for their child regardless of the situation. The children don't learn right from wrong; they learn that no matter what they do, their mom or others will fight to exclude them from any punishment. Unfortunately, that means that the level of misbehavior usually escalates. Situations can worsen and the end result could lie with the police department and the court system. If only parents or guardians had allowed the child to take the punishment, learn from the situation, and move on to better and more acceptable behavior. After a certain point, you may have lost a child—one who is expelled from school and begins moving through the revolving door of the juvenile system. What a waste!

Part of life is learning how to deal with different kinds of people. Not everyone is going to treat you fairly, but you have to learn how to work with them. The school can be the first place students learn this lesson in interpersonal relationships. They also learn that not everyone will be your friend, some people can't be trusted, and when you treat people the way you wish to be treated, it feels good. Unfortunately, some students only learn the mantra repeated at home, such as:

> "What's in it for me?" "How dare she/he touch my child?" "What do you expect from a white/black/Hispanic/woman, man (put in your own stereotype) teacher?"

I have always believed that a child learns what he/she experiences. Living with adults who are prejudiced, foul-mouthed, nicotine-or alcohol-addicted, unappreciative or suspicious of education will lead these once-innocent young people along the same paths. However, some students manage to overcome the negative influences in their lives, and that is the reason many teachers continue in very challenging job situations. They hope to reach those "odds-stacked-against-them" students and make a difference in their lives. Are all teachers perfect and unprejudiced? Of course not, but most would not have entered the teaching profession if they didn't have a caring attitude for and interest in children. Those who get in for the wrong reasons, don't last long.

So parents—please work with us to present a united front for your child. Keep in touch with your child's teacher(s). While you have one or more children at home, we have many more in the classroom. Some years my roll book contained 130 or more names. Check with the source—a telephone call or e-mail to the teacher will allow you to know personal information that will help you at home. Yes, you saw your child working on homework, but did you know that it wasn't turned in for a grade? Begin writing notes that the teacher will sign and return. That way you will know whether assignments made it to class, and what the score was on the last quiz or test, and when the next one is scheduled. If the teacher doesn't respond to your attempts to communicate, keep trying or let the principal know. When parents and teachers work together, the student success rate should improve. In the long run, your son or daughter will definitely be the winner in that type of educational situation. In conclusion, those parents who told their child, "Your teacher wouldn't have taken the time to call me if something wasn't wrong. What is it?" have my lasting thanks!

"Every kid is one caring adult away from being a success story."
—Josh Shipp

TWO VOICES AS ONE...FOR YOU

Education is a vital part of a child's life. It takes involvement from all sides of the "educational triangle"—student, parent, teacher—to ensure success. In this part of your child's life, parental involvement begins with day one of pre-school and ends when your son or daughter completes his/her education.

Food for thought: "An ounce of prevention is worth a pound of cure." Would you rather sit in the classroom with your child or in the courtroom?

TEN YEARS LATER

Deidre's Voice:

Parents, we are living in perilous times! There are so many negative images and messages that plague our youth on a daily basis it may seem that you fighting a losing battle. Therefore, I want to stress to **ALL** parents how you definitely are in serious warfare with the music and movie industry of this 21st century. Everywhere you look young people believe that what they see with their eyes and hear with their ears on a daily basis is reality and an excellent example for how to live out their lives. Too many of them desire to live this fantasy without even knowing that rappers and rockers alike do not actually live the life they dress like and sing about when performing on TV and at concerts. It really is all a colossal show in order to make money and get the young people sold on an image and an idol. Our youth constantly listen to these rap, rock and R&B stars whose lyrics fill their immature minds with images that can pull them so far from their true identity and purpose. Stolen identities really began in the 1980s with the invention of the walkman and the idea of individuality. "I, me, and mine" took on a totally new meaning with each person being able to listen to his or her own music or "jam" on his or her own time wherever they wanted. Songs like "Girls Just Want To Have Fun" by Cyndi Lauper, "Nasty" by Janet Jackson, Madonna's "Material Girl," "We Don't Need No Education" by Pink Floyd, and the Beastie Boys encouraging you to "Fight For Your Right (to party)" all seemed to help start a downward spiral for teens. Hip, new, colorful and expensive headgear called "beats" are worn by many youth almost constantly and encourage them to be isolated, tough, violent, and nonchalant. Movies add images to these lyrics—violent, profanity-laden, sexual images with a wide cast of characters. All of this information overload damages our youth and makes it more difficult for you to parent your child. Some parents may be fortunate enough to have motivated, intelligent, and morally sound children, who for the most part, make the right choices and are obedient by nature. But a majority of children become easily influenced by their peers and the surrounding pop or sub cultures as they enter their teenage years. If you have strong hopes of being effective with helping your children be successful in school and in life, they have to remain grounded or go back to the basics. These basics include God and His way.

Anyone who has raised a child knows that children have to be told over and over what is right and what is wrong. However, society has gotten so far into subjective relativism that too many parents no longer want to draw a line in the sand and stand for right. Parents should be the ones who clearly state and live before their children what is right and what is wrong. Sadly, we live in a time when no one wants to declare that wrong and right still emphatically exist. Equally as sad is the fact that those of us who know the truth about the need to have and live by a specific standard are criticized or seen as fanatical for being so narrow-minded. Just think about how important the directions north, south, east, west, turn left, and go right are when you're traveling. Without those simple directions, travelers could be hopelessly lost. Every parent has been given specific directions as well and has also been given the choice whether or not to follow them. Do not leave your children without the directions they need to successfully navigate this life. As parents, you need to be reminded that "there is a way that may seem right to every man, but the end of that way may lead to death and destruction" (Proverbs 14:12). Parents have been instructed to make time for our children each day. You should tell them when to go to bed, when to wake up, and as much as possible each day about who they are, and Whose they are. Children need to be told that you love them, and they need to be told about the source of your love for them. Do not let the TV, cell phone, computer, or their friends be their main source of information on a daily basis. They need to hear from you more now than ever before in our history. Parents have the right to show tough love by setting limits and boundaries. Please do make spot-checks on their rooms, phones, computers and the clothes they wear. At times these actions will cause them to become angry with you and tell you how much they hate you, but eventually they graduate and leave home. If you have done the training and not allowed BET, MTV, and the numerous movie channels to be the main voice in your child's ear, you will reap the rewards in due season. No child or parent is perfect, but as a parent you must do the very best you can towards your child or children. Parents have been admonished to "train up a child in the way they should go" (Proverbs 22:6). Training involves routine, drills, lectures, lessons, demonstrations, etc. The more you train them, the better off they will be. There are many resources available for parents via workshops, classes, books and websites. Make sure you utilize all materials and any other available assets as best you can, but please do not forget the best manual ever written for parents to use, THE BIBLE.

"Train up a child in the way he should go, and when he is old, he will not depart from it."—Proverbs 22:6

Sue's Voice:

Many educators would love to change the parameters of their teaching profession. I can't tell you how many times I have heard them say, "If I could only lock myself and my students away from superintendents, administrators, and parents and JUST TEACH, what a great life it would be." As in many careers, those people who are not directly involved in the day-to-day process take up a lot of time and effort on your part. This drains your focus from the primary client—your students. They alone should have the best part of you. In this perfect world of teaching, you would incorporate the lesson plan to include more than just your blueprint of raw data . . . you could add items that popped up spontaneously and slide them in for a "teachable moment" lesson. Students would help determine what is important for that particular day. Hot news items in the social studies curriculum, new math concepts just introduced through internet connections, science discoveries from around the world, newly introduced age-appropriate novels and short stories. The list could go on and on. What freedom and what excitement! The end result has to be better than regimented day by day test-driven data and endless paper work proving you are teaching to that test. UGHHHHH! How many teachers have left the classroom because of it and miss the students and the true educational process? Oops! It seems I have returned to Chapter II. Let me focus on the current topic at hand.

Parents, teachers will never replace you. You are your child's first teacher, and the home is their first classroom, for good or bad. This is not a contest; it is a partnership. That darling infant is growing into a person day by day, and experience by experience. All of us want him/her to make us proud. As a parent, I understand that one of the hardest things to do is to allow your child to take his/her "lumps," and not fix the situation for them. Consequences of our actions are best taught by experiencing them. Children quickly learn that painful results should not be repeated, and most work to change their choices for the better. However, they have to experience these bad results to understand the necessity of avoiding them in the future. When you get in the way, none of that happens. I stand by what I originally said in Chapter III. We need you on the education team as an ally, not an adversary. Communication with teachers will help you be prepared to take the hard line with your child. Remember, you are focusing on the end result. An entitled child grows up to expect things handed to him or her. Too much protection as they grow can cause a real handicap in real-world situations. This world is fast becoming a "fend for your-self" environment. Will teachers, coaches, college professors, or employers make excuses for your offspring, or is the reality a failing grade, exclusion from the team, a lost semester, or the loss of a job? Is your child prepared for that? If not, whose fault is it?

CHAPTER IV

Teacher to Student

"Choice, not chance, determines destiny."
—Anonymous

Voice I:

I want to say to all young ladies and gentlemen who are still in school, "Keep it real!" As I have said to many young people already, "Just be yourself." In reality, the majority of students want so badly to be accepted by their friends in school and other peers they come in contact with on a regular basis, that they assume someone else's identity. That may be just fine as long as you're not doing things that go against your own morals, values, and goals. I strongly suggest that you get to know who you really are. When you are away from your friends, think about yourself:

> What do you like?
> What do you want to do with your life?
> Do you really think that smoking is cool, or sex is great when
>   no one else is there to influence you?
> Do you actually like loud and talkative people, or do you
>   prefer a more quiet crowd?

You may discover the peers you want to accept you are not anything like the real you. Once you make this discovery, you can feel less pressure to fit In with that crowd, and find friends more like yourself. True friendship should be mostly fun, not mainly frustrating.

Like most teenagers, my daughter began to question the values and teachings of our home. She began to wonder if she believed in God for herself, or was it because mom and dad always told her that He was real. She began to want to wear tight, revealing clothes, saying it was what she wanted to do, and not because everyone was doing it. She asked if she always had to listen to gospel music, or could she listen to R & B as well? These and other similar questions began to come up more and more as she left middle school and entered high school. My response to her and to you is that to begin to question and seek your own identity is normal, and you will have to provide the final answers to those questions. To help you do this, watch what happens to the people with positive attitudes, the ones who study, don't use drugs or "drink and drive," versus those who are constantly negative, experiment with illegal drugs, refuse to study, and consume alcohol before they get behind the wheel. Let what you see and know about others help you decide. Remember Michael Jordan didn't become a basketball icon by drinking alcohol, talking and acting "bad," and using drugs. However, Len Bias, college star and the NBA's #2 overall draft pick, tried cocaine once and died in June of 1986 before he ever played one professional game. His death was a shocking example of the reality of drug experimentation.

Students who put name brand dressing and socializing above studying and grades are setting themselves up for failure or a less productive lifestyle. When education is not valuable to you, you will come to school just to look good and talk to your friends. Eventually, you will come out of school a dummy—how smart is that? Think about this for a moment: have any of you who put so much emphasis on wearing name brand clothes above studying and good grades ever received a commission check for advertising Nike, Tommy Hilfiger, Timberland, and FUBU? If you want to look good, then look good. Just have the brains to back up the good looks!

You will learn that bad things happen to good people, and bad people seemingly have it good. This is a fact of life. The greatest book ever written says "it rains on the just and the unjust," so each person will have hard times in this life no matter how good he/she is. Significant to that truth is how we go through the bad times. Will you turn to drugs, alcohol, or sex to appease your hurt or will you turn to God and your family and friends who care? Can you look in the mirror and honestly say, "I like the person looking back at me?" Will you feel good about yourself whether you have one friend or twenty? Once again, I want to stress to you that you must be true to yourself. Find a way to do that and just stay "real."

Many of you have read S. E. Hinton's The Outsiders and remember Johnny's character telling Ponyboy to "stay gold" as Johnny lay dying. Gold will still be gold, even when it has gone through fire. To your parents and others who care for you, you are gold and precious. Stay true to their teachings and don't let others change you from a precious gem to a ruined stone. If you can live with your decisions, that is all that matters. Regret is a painful experience, and some decisions change our lives forever and we can never take them back.

In conclusion, remember to make the most out of your life. You need to make every moment count because tomorrow is not promised to you, so make today your best day. Choose to be positive and treat people the way you want to be treated. It is so important that you set goals for your life and then work to reach them. Today is your chance to make it all start to happen. I just know you can succeed if you keep trying. Never give up or stop trying to make yourself better. Keep improving yourself until the day you die. Now get ready, get set, and go do it!

Voice II:

During my years as a middle school teacher, I have taught children who range in age from ten to fourteen or older, representing the whole spectrum of academic ability and achievement. Every year there are times that I feel the need to speak to my students on a variety of topics. Individually and as a class, I counsel them because it's not easy being a student today. The world is a much more complicated place than when I was a teenager, and today's youth are faced with many more distractions and problems.

Our culture today is definitely not representative of life in the "Ozzie and Harriet" or "Leave It To Beaver" time period. Fewer students are growing up with an intact family consisting of one mother, one father, and one or more siblings. Single parents struggle to financially support their children, sometimes working more than one job and having little personal time to spend with their sons or daughters. Television programs present murder, profanity, disrespect to authority figures, and immoral behavior at all times of the day and night. Music videos show lewd dancing and present lyrics that do not encourage young people to view the opposite sex with respect. The news is filled with depressing events from around the world and just down the street. More and more students come to school with identified and unidentified learning problems. Some come hungry not only for food, but also for attention. It's no wonder that many students are not succeeding in today's classrooms. In this chapter I want to speak to the world of students who will never enter my classroom and talk to them as though they have:

"By the time you reach middle school, you are beginning to have a mind of your own. Think about how many times you have disagreed lately with the adults in your life about music, fashions, friends, or even food. At this age you are trying to find yourself and discover who you are. It is very important for you to realize that your life as a teenager will be filled with times when you must make decisions. Some decisions are as simple as which pair of jeans to select from your closet; others are so important that they will impact your future life. Should you listen to your friends who are, for the most part, just as confused as you are about what is happening to their bodies, their thoughts, and their lives? How about the "cool" kids or the popular ones— would they give you good advice? To whom do you turn when everything seems to be going crazy? Most of you, if you're fortunate, have at least one caring adult who has invested a lot in you. Think of it— they have provided a roof over your head, food on your table, clothes on your back and in your closet, perhaps a computer and internet hookup, CD player, and many other things. I'm about to mention the unmentionable: consider trusting your parents' or guardians' advice. They have already lived through your age and have experienced a lot of what you are going through right now. They care about you and don't want to see you hurt. Why would they give you bad advice? Your friends or the other young people at school don't have the same emotional attachment to you that these adults in your life do. So please share with them and seek out their advice. Other adults care about you too. A teacher or counselor that you feel comfortable talking to at school, a Scout or YMCA leader, or a Sunday school teacher could help you with problems as well.

Let me suggest another area of guidance and help. Hopefully, you have been introduced to the One who loves you most and wants to guide you throughout your life. If this concept is new to you, let me give you some very good news—you have a Heavenly Father who loves you and has a plan for your life. In Psalms 139 we are told that God knew us before we were born and wants to guide us daily and throughout our lives. He wants only good for us but will allow us to choose our path through life. Learning about this God of the Ages and His rules for life will definitely help you in making those important everyday choices.

Our society is good at pointing fingers or blaming others for personal mistakes. Regardless of your home situation—two parents, one parent, step-parents, guardians, foster parents, or relatives—you are responsible for the choices you make. You cannot blame anyone else if you choose to not complete your school work or study, run with the wrong type of friends, or get involved with cigarettes, drugs, alcohol, or sexual behavior. As motivational speaker Drew Brown says, 'You are the only person you will ever wake up with for the rest of your life.' Make sure that the person looking back at you from the mirror is one who makes you proud, not ashamed. Don't point to anyone else for your mistakes. The Lord gave you a brain—use it! Think before you act, trust those who care for you, and do your best in everything you try. Some chances will only be offered once. You don't want to look back years later and regret passing up a wonderful opportunity.

The bottom line is this: <u>You</u> alone are responsible for your education. Education equals the power not only to qualify for certain jobs, but also to live a more blessed life. No one would turn down a town home in a good neighborhood to live in the slums, but that could be the result when you say 'no' to school and a better education. Dr. Martin L. King, Jr., lived his life trying to open doors that had been closed for many. Teachers come to work every day just for you. They know the material and simply want to help you along the path to success. Don't slam the door to that path by refusing to be a responsible learner. Every day is a new beginning; use each day wisely because you will never get it back again!"

TWO VOICES AS ONE...FOR YOU

You may not realize it, but school is just one small portion of your life. Set goals, decide now what you want to do in life, and "go for it." Remember that being successful in school will help you be successful in life. Bill Gates, one of the richest men in the world because of his knowledge and inventive work with computers, once said, "Get to know and make friends with the nerds in your school—one day they may be your bosses!" Put equal emphasis on your looks and academic ability. Being "cool and cute," but in reality, "dumb and despondent" is such a waste of your life. As a student, you must understand that ignorance is more expensive than knowledge because "not knowing" will affect your potential earnings for the rest of your life. It is possible to look good, be popular, and be smart at the same time. <u>A well-rounded person is a fantastic package!</u>

TEN YEARS LATER

Deidre's Voice:

"Money, money, money, money . . . MONNNEEYYY" are the first words to a popular tune sang in 1973 by The O'Jays. YouTube will play it for you if you haven't heard it already, but chances are, you may have heard it in a recent Crown Royal commercial featuring NBA legend Dr. J. How sad, prophetic, and truthful that song seems to ring even today because "For the Love of Money" so many teenagers are lying, stealing, cheating, and killing in order to experience a life full of material wealth and things, regardless of the cost—their lives, relationships, or future dreams and aspirations. Even sadder, many teens want to either look, sing, and act like Beyonce, rap like Jay Z or Lil Wayne, or be among the very small 1% who play at the NBA or

NFL level. Saddest of all, none of these people have chosen to use their gifts and talents to the glory of God!

Your career choice should not include being a rapper, singer, or ball player just because TV sends the message to you that you have to do one of the above to be liked, respected, popular, or rich. Young men, when you dress like many rappers by wearing your pants halfway off your behinds, it causes you to have to walk like you are a slave in bondage on a chain gang because one hand is always locked on to having to hold up your pants. This look is neither cool nor smart. Young ladies, when you wear clothes so tight that they look like they were painted on permanently, it sends a message. Sadly, Beyonce dresses like that on a stage to attract and perform, but you dress like her and other top performers, and walk around your schools, super-markets, and local stores thinking you look cute, but in reality, you are saying that you are easy to obtain because you don't mind display-ing what you have for free. Young people, do not put tattoos all over your bodies because you see star performers and athletes doing that. They are making lots of money right now, and they will not care until later when their money runs dry. However, you have to go to college, interview and get a real job one day soon. If you live past the age of thirty, body tattoos, excess piercing and dressing like the stars make you look extremely odd. What is so popular today looks funny and outdated later. When you alter your appearance so much, you really begin to look mechanical and fake. Teenagers, you cannot be some-one else no matter how hard you try. You must seek to be who God made you to be, and you were made for greatness no matter if that greatness is for a few people or for the masses.

Ten years ago, I admonished students to "Keep It Real" by discover-ing who they really are and being true to that person. Ten years later, my message is still the same, but I want to suggest to you some more specific instructions on how to really discover and be yourself. The definition of "Keeping It Real" that I want you to think about is to simply JUST be yourself. First of all, you were born and created for a purpose (Jeremiah 29:11). If you are here, it is by God's design and not a mistake or accident regardless of how you were conceived or who your parents are. Society may tell you that lie until you begin to question why you were even born. However, you have to believe your Creator, who said that before you were formed in your mother's womb, He already knew you. (Jeremiah 1:5) That means you were in His mind and heart until you were ready to be born and live in the 21st Century.

Never before in history have youth your age been able to influence or be influenced by so many, so fast, and so far. During the 1960s, Walt Disney created a theme and ride in his park based on the Sherman Brothers' song, "It's a Small World After All." Disney decided to have a major attraction that would feature models of children from all over the world with the "small world" song translated in as many different languages as possible. It was just an idea then that became a major attraction at the famous Disneyland and Disney World theme parks. Today, however, the world has become so small or so global that you can actually play games with some teenager in China, or Skype on the phone to a friend in the United Kingdom, or even send electronic mail to other youth in Africa or Australia. Indeed, you live in one of the most exciting times in history.

Contrary to all these positive developments is the negative side; you also live in one of the most exposed and dangerous times in our history which makes it even more vital for you to understand who you are, and why you are here. You must fully accept and agree with the powerful truth that you were put here for a purpose. If you wish to discover that purpose, you can begin by carefully assessing and self-evaluating your skills, qualities, talents and gifts:

> What do you really enjoy doing?
>
> What are you good at doing?
>
> What are you naturally drawn to do for fun or relaxation?
>
> What do others tell you are good at or what are you known for doing well?
>
> Who do you hurt for or feel a natural compassion towards?
>
> With whom are you most likely to spend time, feel comfortable and be yourself?
>
> Have you considered the type of personality you have?
>
> Do you ever write down and discuss with others your likes, dislikes, strengths, skills, gifts, and talents?
>
> Are you funny by nature, serious, or a combination of both?
>
> Do you thrive on socializing with others or find solace and peace being alone but not in a depressed way?

The more you are able to think about the answers to all of these questions and other questions like these, the better you can start thinking about why you were made that special way and feel good about yourself no matter what anyone else may say or think about you. Think about yourself the same way David did in Psalm 139:14 when he declared how he was "fearfully and wonderfully made." That is the way you must think of yourself in order to be motivated to seek out your purpose in life. Thinking positive thoughts about yourself on a regular basis can be difficult for you to do because you tend to compare yourself to others. Just remember, the Bible is and always has been the standard by which you should measure yourself. Keep practicing; you will get better at discovering who you really are and why you were put here on earth, "for such a time as this." My pastor, Bishop V. McLaughlin, often says, just "Do You." He means do not want to try to be like anybody else. You will be most miserable and waste precious moments out of your own life trying to copy or be someone else. Copy-cat living keeps you bound to living a lie and causes so many people in your life to miss out on the gifts God invested in you to be a blessing to others. Someone needs to know the real you in order to become who they really are. An extrovert may need an introvert to help give balance and vice versa. It is a fact that we may have similar gifts, talents, and personalities, but no two people are just alike. Our fingerprints confirm that simple truth. Would there be the same level of enjoyment and excitement in a simple game of basketball if every single player was Kobe Bryant's height, or everybody played the game like LeBron James or looked like Chris "Birdman" Anderson? Variety is really the spice of life, and your sphere of influence is needed in a positive way among your circle of friends and acquaintances. You are the greatest person you will ever know. You must know yourself in order to love yourself because you can never live life without yourself. Any and every place you go, "YOU" are right there. I want you to know that you were born for this. "This" is whatever you do best naturally and with whom you enjoy spending time. That natural attraction is a major clue for you to use to help discover your purpose.

Also, you must keep on going to school and stay in school . . . until you graduate. Do not drop out early because as a teenager, you should be in school, and not hanging out in the streets, getting high, getting drunk, or breaking the law for "fun." Make the best grades possible and ask for a tutor at your school if you need the extra help. Take the initiative to use YouTube for something other than downloading songs full of lies and lewd behavior. Study hard, take the ACT, SAT, and practice tests as early as possible. Research colleges you desire to attend and set your goals to meet their entrance criteria. If you do not get accepted by your first choice, try others and keep searching until you find the college that is the exact fit for you. Get the highest G.P.A. and take advanced or college courses early, if possible. You will also need to have more than one back-up plan like the military, trade school, or community college in order to get your grades up to an acceptable average for the larger university that was really your first choice. Remember, you were created by the most intelligent and the only infinite designer of all, God. Therefore, you all have some level of intelligence, and you must continue to use what you have been given to the best of your ability. You must do your personal best and move forward with purpose. Educate your mind, improve your skills and attitudes as necessary, but use the Bible as your standard for living a sound moral and ethical lifestyle. Right and Wrong is just as much a reality as following laws or breaking them. Many people do not want to identify what sin is, but if you steal their wallet, they automatically know that you did wrong.

While you are on this journey to discover yourself, do not believe the lie of our time known as subjective relativism that allows what everyone believes to be right in their own eyes. There is still the one true standard that God has given us to live by daily. The Bible is the universal truth for all people, for all times. It never changes and will not lead you in the wrong way. When you fail at a specific task or you meet an obstacle, do not give up. Pray, ask, and seek God for direction. He promises to guide you when you ask (Proverbs 3:5-7). As God begins to reveal the real you, you must "Do You," and you will discover many more interesting things about yourself that you never knew or thought possible. As you continue to live, grow, mature and "Do You," you must also choose to use all your gifts and talents to the Glory of God because He gave it all to you anyway. At each level of discovery and growth, the choice to glorify Him will always be yours.

Sue's Voice:

This is the season for prom. It amazes me how much time, effort, and money is put into one evening. The right dress and shoes, matching tux and tie, hair and nails, dinner reservations, perhaps a limo—and then it's all over, except for the photos and memories. Don't get me wrong, prom is a rite of passage and usually a wonderful evening. However, I can't help but wonder what would happen if students (and their parents) put as much time and effort into preparing for their futures as they do for a one-time event.

I have been privileged to reconnect with some of my former students as they live their adult lives and have been amazed at what they have already accomplished. They are now college professors, manage their own businesses, are foreign travelers, teachers, hospital caregivers, government insiders, professional athletes, pastors, speak several languages, go on yearly mission trips, and at least one has his doctorate (!)—you get the idea. I have also attended more than my share of funerals or read about jail time for students who followed the wrong path. Teachers never really know who is sitting in their classroom. The future can be bright or devastating.

As you can tell by reading Deidre's 'Ten Years Later,' she is a counselor and minister whose love for young people causes her to tell it like it is. Working, planning, testing, and pushing students to achieve their very best is in her DNA along with the need to preach the gospel to any who will listen. I thoroughly agree with every word of her advice to you. As you move into high school, your level of independence should grow with every year. By the time you graduate, you should be ready to step out on your own into the next area of your life. Leaving for college, trade school, the military or the work world without knowing how to manage your time, money, and schedule is guaranteed to cause you nothing but heartache and frustration. Sleeping in longer instead of attending that 8:00 class, spending your money without taking into consideration gasoline needs, or forgetting to pay rent and other bills because budgeting your income has never been part of your life experiences are examples of the lack of real life skills that will cause you all kinds of trouble. These are skills that you will need to have to survive the real world. Life is out there for you, which is such an exciting thought, but it requires a whole new set of rules that you should follow.

We each have a set amount of time on this earth. We can use it for good or not so good, but the choice is ultimately up to us. Education is never a bad thing. Your younger years are meant to pave the way for your ultimate future. Don't waste the minutes, hours, or days. Put effort into what is going to be YOUR LIFE! Check out the options after high school during your eighth or ninth grade years: a two-year college, trade school, military, four-year university, work experience in retail, construction, plumbing, etc. Have a plan for what you want to do, or life will happen to you. It is so true. Many of my former students have returned to visit and have told me that I was so right to encourage them to work harder. But they had to experience the downside of life's experiences before they realized it. I would like for you to avoid those bad times. That beautiful prom dress didn't just appear; neither did the memorable evening. It took planning, work, savings, and time to make everything happen. Your education and future life deserves the same investment on your part. Plan now to succeed later - I wish you the very best.

"Everything you do is based on the choices you make. It is not your parents, your past relationships, your job, the economy, the weather, an argument, or your age that is to blame. You and only you are responsible for every decision and choice you make. Period."
—Susan Abrams Milligan

CHAPTER V

Overworked, Underpaid, and Misunderstood

"A teacher affects eternity;
he can never tell where his influence stops."
—Henry Adams

Voice I:

Notably, the teaching profession is one of the most honorable and influential of jobs, but not all Americans realize that. They also don't understand the problems with some of our flawed educational systems that are unduly challenging teachers as well as students.

It is a known fact that our schools are of great concern to many people. We often hear about efforts being made to help promote change for the better by our lawmakers and school officials. Yet sometimes, the very people working towards these changes tend to be, in my opinion, the wrong people. This is because some of the people making the decisions for the current teachers have been out of the classroom for long periods of time, or worse still, have never taught at all. The question is how can they know what is best or what is needed? I feel strongly that we need to stop putting Band-aids on our problems within the educational system and instead perform major surgery to fix the wounds.

We are facing some serious educational issues in our country today. For example, we are living in the 21st century and involved with a high tech era that is rapidly growing, forcing us to compete with other countries. Will our students, who are also our future, be prepared? Perhaps it is time to revamp our entire system. Long gone are the days when one teacher stood and taught multiple ages and grade levels.

Laura Ingalls Wilder of the *Little House on the Prairie* series could do this well because the caliber of students was so different then. However, today one person meeting the educational, psychological, and emotional needs of 27+ children seems ridiculous. Sometimes not having enough textbooks for each student or even a classroom in which to prepare and teach is a reality for some in the profession. Not to mention the fact that daily some students come to school with guns or drugs or are totally uninterested in learning. This is a new millennium that presents teachers with many new and challenging problems.

For these problems there are no easy answers, but we are still not close to addressing all of the issues. This is because society has failed to consult the experts in this matter, the teachers who are involved on a day-to-day basis. Some people say, "Teachers are underpaid and I couldn't or wouldn't do their jobs—give them a raise!" But that's a simple way out. I believe it is time for society as a whole to become more knowledgeable and get involved with the education process. Each adult needs to feel responsible for helping to educate our students because, as President Herbert Hoover said years ago, "Children are our most valuable natural resource." Yet we don't seem to want to involve ourselves with really preparing them even though we know how important they are to our future.

Some students will never make it on just "book knowledge;" they may need to pursue a vocation. What would be wrong with some students earning a vocational diploma instead of being passed, but not promoted, through the system year after year? Many teachers object to these "administrative promotions," but are often overruled and then ultimately blamed for students not graduating with basic skills. I feel we need to have more vocational, technical trade, college prep, and life skills instruction in every school system where students can learn a skill or trade so they can be taught to be an asset to society and not a burden. Such schools would enable a student to achieve and succeed in areas that are excluded in most current systems. Each student should have a choice in his/her future plans and not be forced to fit into a curriculum that is not of their choosing. The major misunderstanding in most school systems today is assuming that all students must follow an academic track in high school to prepare for college. For some students this process is similar to trying to force a square peg into a round hole because not all students are college material. Robert White, a great educator, once said, "Every child needs to feel success." His statement embodies the core of my philosophy of education and leads me to focus more on the question of how then do we help every child to be successful? We do this by addressing their needs and not ours. If society does not allow some students to succeed outside the academic realm, they will fail within it.

Students today are getting mixed messages. The school expects our youth to attend class after class, listening to lecture after lecture, be quiet, take notes, and make good grades. Yet everything else in society tells them to express themselves, have fun, and be spontaneous. Nintendo, X-Box, DVDs, CDs, and computers have replaced kickball, street hockey, family nights out, and "red light, green light, 1-2-3." With less outdoor and physical recreation time, it is no wonder that teachers have more discipline problems, need to counsel and help students work out personal situations, and find themselves filling out loads of paperwork—all of which cut into actual teaching time.

Our society needs to understand that it's not just the schools or the teacher that affect our students. The homes from which they come can also influence the children who find their way into our classrooms. Many moms and dads in two-parent homes have little time to spend there because their budget or lifestyle requires two incomes. Single parent homes leave many students home alone from the critically important hours of 3:00 p.m. until 11:00 p.m. Who is home to enforce homework time, house rules, and train the child in the way he should go? Even when two parents are in the home, the demands of today's living with church, clubs, civic groups, recreation leagues, grocery store lines, mall shopping, and the excessive number of social obligations (birthday parties, anniversaries, showers, etc) allow children too much "alone time." Many times they don't have to conform to rules at home, but are expected to follow rigid rules at school. The teachers and principals become the enforcers with parents many times not understanding why their child is being disciplined and treated "unfairly."

It is a sad day when one can make millions shooting a ball or just throwing one while a teacher may have to work two jobs just to make ends meet. This may send the message to our youth that education is really not important to make a good living. Likewise, it keeps teachers demoralized as they get the message, "Just keep them in class, help them pass the state required tests, and we will pay you something for your trouble." Have we mixed up our priorities in the pursuit of material possessions? Have we forgotten that investing in human lives was and still is one of our greatest responsibilities? Or could the problem lie with the fact that the majority of Americans just don't understand?

Voice II:

Who in the world would go to college for four years to earn a degree in one or more specific subjects, and then continue on for another year to acquire their certification? Education majors—teachers— that's who. Then after completing five years of higher education, these men and women of all ages, races, and backgrounds enter the "real world" of students, administrators, parents, computer grade programs, lesson plans, deadlines, standardized testing, telephone and face-to-face conferences, meetings, blame and accusations. They probably ask themselves, "What have I gotten myself into?"

The teaching profession is a sometimes challenging, but often very rewarding career. However, those on the outside have no idea of how difficult it can be to attempt to motivate, teach, test, remediate, retest, and grade students from age five to nineteen in class sizes ranging from 10 to 35 or more students at a time. Those teachers who excel at their job usually begin their day at least half an hour before the students arrive, teach one class all day in various subjects, one subject all day to five or more classes, or a variety of classes to even more than five sets of students. They have very few bathroom or rest breaks throughout the day. At lunchtime, they gulp down their food while sometimes supervising children, dashing to the copy machine, helping students with makeup work, or answering telephone messages. Then they stay after the children have left for the day to tutor certain students, enter grades in the computer, plan for tomorrow or next week, and attend faculty meetings, conferences, or workshops. If this weren't enough, most teachers end their day at school by loading up all the papers, projects, or mail they haven't been able to complete or read in a big carry-all bag to take home. Getting through this bag might take an additional one to two hours, and then they can look forward to doing it all again the next day. The teaching profession can definitely be described as one in which the employees are overworked, and those entering it can expect to earn the whopping starting salary of $28,000+ a year (2005 sample salary scale). Teachers are underpaid!

Teachers across the country in all disciplines with all age groups are characteristically underpaid. Somehow this low paycheck seems to demonstrate a lack of respect for the profession. I've listened to talk radio or read articles criticizing teachers, with some stating that they are paid enough already. These pundits talk about the three months off every summer (actually much less than that), the short work day (8:30 2:30—not quite!), and the fact that teachers really don't have to work very hard. I just have to laugh through my frustration, but actually such statements are sadly out of touch with reality. One internet story I read told the tale of a derisive parent who said that teachers deserve no more pay than the amount a babysitter would earn. Once the math was completed, the amazed parent realized that paying only 50 cents per hour per student would total a yearly salary for some of over $100,000—a sum no classroom teacher I know currently earns. Basic babysitter pay from the 1960s would multiply the average teacher salary almost three times! Do teachers deserve more pay? I remember listening to parents after they had volunteered in the school for a day or two. I would see them shake their heads in amazement at how much teachers have to accomplish every day and see their disappointment at the attitudes, disrespect, or just plain apathy shown by some misguided students. Usually they make some sort of comment, such as: "I don't know how you do it; the public ought to see what teachers have to experience with other people's children!" Those volunteers appreciate us and think we deserve more money because they have been on the front line with us. A saying I found on a refrigerator magnet states another truism: "Parents appreciate teachers the most when it rains all weekend." Let me repeat it once more—teachers are underpaid!

You cannot truly understand another person's perspective unless you have experienced their situation firsthand (Ch. VII—*Two Voices As One*). For that reason alone, teachers are misunderstood. Some parents don't understand that we teach more than just their child, and cannot give Susie or Hector extra-special treatment. Teachers have to be seen by their students as fair, someone who treats all students equally. Unless an identified condition, physical affliction, or disease deems this child worthy of special treatment, a teacher has to apply classroom rules equally to each and every child in his/her class. Deadlines are another area that some parents find difficult to understand. If a project or an assignment is due by a certain date, then points are deducted from the grade for work that is turned in later. If you know that there is a conflict (appointment, trip, etc.), communicate that problem early and then misunderstandings can be avoided.

A teacher can be misunderstood by his/her administrator if the lines of communication are not kept open. I have heard horror stories about domineering and dictatorial principals who don't enter the classroom to see what and how the children are learning, but come to "nit-pick" and check off every little detail on bulletin boards, learning centers, and lesson plans. These types of people don't lead; they dominate and they make the teaching profession a living hell for the teachers at that particular school. They need to go because they do no one any good! Thankfully, I have not experienced any principals like the ones described above. I have worked with ten or more principals during my teaching career, and although each had different styles, they were all caring, open, and willing to listen. Possibly our positive relationships were due to the fact that I was a hard worker doing my job, but I have to give them credit for being people that I was willing to follow because their demands were fair and impacted positively on the students I taught.

The most misunderstanding sometimes comes from the central office—those whom Deidre and I characterize as working in the "ivory towers." These people never experience our lives firsthand, but have no problem whatsoever in coming up with more and more criteria and paperwork for us to complete. Superintendents, assistant superintendents, curriculum leaders, and others are so far removed from the classroom that there are many instances where misunderstandings can readily occur. My suggestion for the problem is to require everyone—even the superintendent—to periodically enter the classroom to plan, teach, grade, discipline, and communicate to parents, not just for a day, but for 3-4 weeks. Once they have been reminded of the reality of the "real world," communication would be reinstated and more understanding of the teacher's situation regained.

The media really seems to have the teaching situation skewed. Numerous articles and talk shows have attacked the public school system and unqualified teachers who are "failing our students." As long as students are passed to the next grade year after year without acquiring the reading, writing, and math skills necessary to master that grade level's work, the system will be broken. Many states have these types of situational rules or allow parents to manipulate existing criteria so that their child is promoted regardless of low test scores or failing report card grades. Occasionally, the superintendent or others will make an executive decision to silence a complaining parent and allow a retained student to move to the next grade. Middle school students reading on a third grade level move on to sixth or seventh grade unable to understand the textbooks or media info, and continue to be unwilling to do the work because they haven't had to in the past. It's not just the schools and the teachers who are part of this seemingly broken system; the parents, students, administrators, legislators, and others share in the blame. However, the result is the same—too many students who lack the basic skills to succeed or move to the next level. Accountability is being focused solely on one side of this problem. I have always maintained that the teacher—me—is only one-third (1/3) of the problem or the solution. The rest of this "school math problem," the student and the parent, make or break the education equation. This situation can also be explained in an analogy of a three-legged stool. Each leg is crucially important if the stool is to support any weight. Remove any leg, and the stool collapses.

For those and other reasons, teachers are often misunderstood. However, many of us wouldn't do anything else for a living and agree with Robert Frost when he said, "I am not a teacher, but an awakener." We find that the hard work is worth it when we see the positive expression on a student's face when he/she finally catches onto a concept and smiles broadly, or hear the gratefulness in a parent's voice as they thank us for the extra tutoring we have done for their child. At the end of the day, I feel satisfied because I am a part of one of the most honorable professions—I am a teacher!

TWO VOICES AS ONE...FOR YOU

America needs to know and realize that we must all accept responsibility for the well-being of our future generations. The teachers and the school system cannot do it all. Education does not begin or end inside the classroom or the school building. It will take a "village" and more to help rear our children. Wake up, America—our children need us! We must stop being blind to their needs as we so selfishly pursue our own. Things do not replace parenting; a telephone, computer, TV, and DVD player cannot raise your child and can interfere with his/her education. What we <u>leave in</u> our children in terms of character, morals, and lessons for life is much more important than what we <u>give to</u> them. This is not a racial thing, a gender thing, or a cultural thing—it is a people thing. We all need to understand that we must come together on some common ground and put our differences aside to work for the good of all of our children. As teacher/astronaut Christa McAuliffe once said, "I teach—I touch the future."

So does society and so do parents.

TEN YEARS LATER

Deidre's Voice:

It's 2014, and America's educational system and its educators still remain one of the most misunderstood professions. I think there are many reasons for this. There never seems to be enough time to get it all done as most of "the powers that be" continue to impose heavy demands on their teachers regarding student achievement and test accountability. In addition to these demands, advanced technology has dominated tremendous amounts of our daily lives with electronic accountability and hand-held "distractors," while many of our schools have not taken that same advanced leap into this current era of technology with its plethora of constant electronic upgrades. Additionally, there is a constant barrage of arts and entertainment via cable TV, satellite radio, and 24-7 news coverage that can capture minute-by-minute events full of violence and other alarming news stories from around the world. The average teacher is competing with stimulation overdrive from all parts of our globe among students who have benefitted from having the latest electronic devices. However, other students in the same classroom setting may have limited access to this same type of information. Classrooms and school districts possessing smart boards, smart/electronic books, computers in every classroom, and multi-purpose visual equipment are still extremely limited to a small percentage of all classrooms.

I believe that now is a really crucial time for teachers to unite and request an audience with our President and Department of Education officials in order to encourage open forums. Perhaps these open and candid discussions can begin in every state asking for and allowing honest input from teachers, parents and the communities in which our schools are located. These open forums should include public, private, and home schools alike because all of our children have basic educational needs across the board. I believe much of the focus needs to be on what we can do in lieu of so many demands for teachers to teach the skills on these state mandated tests regardless of a consistent decrease in test scores. This decline in our nation's overall test statistics has impacted all ethnicities, genders and socio-economic groups. Other important areas an open forum could address include the topics of cultural differences/tolerance and the consistent disparity on standardized test scores between Whites, Asians, and growing minority groups like Blacks and Hispanics. The huge lack of resources available for students and teachers at schools that need improvement, otherwise labeled as "D" or "F" schools, would also prove to be a concern for many individuals to discuss. Another question might be whether or not virtual classes/schools, Duel Enrollment, AP classes and IB programs are meeting the needs for a majority of students or just a select few. "Separate but equal" has now taken on a whole new meaning when it comes to the technology available in some schools districts or classes and not others. All schools need the same or similar technological equipment and resources so that all students are learning on an even playing field. When America can pay professional sports players millions of dollars, and invest perhaps billions in scholarship money to our college athletes, but not make sure every school has the proper facilities and resources it needs to educate our youth, we have a major problem in this country.

We also need more monetary donations from individuals and private corporations to help cover the expense of offering more of a variety in the different types of high schools available to everyone. Businesses will be hiring these students, so they have a vested interesting in giving. Currently, college prep schools and magnet schools are not offered to every child in every school district in the same way. More requirements for parental involvement at the secondary levels need to be put in place for student support. The classroom teacher should not be made to feel the sole responsibility when students continue to fail their state's Standards of Learning benchmark tests and promotional tests. And then there is the salary question—what other means of support are available to help teachers receive a comparable salary to other professions. Research groups need to be set in place to explore and discover how other countries succeed with educating their youth and preparing them for life beyond high school.

Remember the triangle of support for every student includes the teacher, parent, and student. We could add an additional side (now a square!)—that of the administrator. This particular concept could be the starting point for America's open forums entitled "Crisis in the Classroom." Ten years later teachers are still overworked because, underpaid because, and definitely misunderstood because America has seemingly forgotten how every scientist, professor, plumber, electrician, contractor, and even movie star, had to first go through a school system with many different teachers. Some may have been bad, but some were definitely good. I am reminded of the deep impact Maya Angelou's autobiography had on me when I read an excerpt from her *I Know Why the Caged Bird Sings* to my eighth graders. In her life's story, she reflects how Mrs. Flowers changed her life forever because she was her "life-line." I also had several good teachers myself throughout my lifetime, but all teachers make some type of lasting impact on us for good or bad. More positive support for our teachers helps them to become better advocates for all of our children.

Without any more delay, it is time for more teachers to be heard on a large scale before a larger audience! "CHANGE" was the most consistent word President Obama used when he initially ran for office over seven years ago, and now so many people are saying, "Keep your change!" However, I say, "Change must come now or else our educational system and our most valuable human resource—our children—will be broken beyond repair."

Sue's Voice:

Although it's ten years later, I do not see that much has changed in the education arena. The buzzwords are a bit different as it is now the Common Core that is driving teachers and parents a bit crazy at the current time, but the scenario remains the same. The underlying theme just seems to repeat itself: striving to look for the elusive carrot that will solve the dilemma of why our students are not achieving, and continuing to look within the classroom to the teacher or an outdated program as the problem or solution. Will we never understand that the raw student material comes to us in many shapes, sizes, and forms which dramatically affects the educational outcome? However, the school system via the teacher is continually expected to turn out identically shaped and acceptable products—achievers who score higher on tests, raise our rankings among other nations, and make us proud. It reminds me of the famous Albert Einstein quote: "Doing the same things again and again, but expecting different results is a sign of insanity." That is how teachers sometimes feel at the end of the day—insane!

Deidre and I have tried to give you an accurate description of what it is like to be on the front lines of education. Our words could probably be used to describe other professions as well. The people at the top run the show and the underlings try to fulfill their wishes while questioning the rationale, and wondering why they are working so hard to accomplish a goal they feel is a waste of time. However, manufacturing auto parts or filling shelves to better market a product is far different, in my opinion, than educating children. The results of this latter endeavor affect people for their lifetimes. What works for one child may not work for another. It can be a frustrating profession, but such an important one. However, until we have a majority of the parents and children who are just as interested in learning as the school and the teacher, I fear not a lot will change. It is not mean, cruel, or unfair to hold children accountable for their work (or lack of it) and behavior. Their self-esteem will survive punishment at home and school for unacceptable work effort. Habits come from behaviors learned in childhood. Do you really want your son or daughter to become used to doing less than their best?

I recently read an article about Josh Waldron, a young, dynamic, award-winning Virginia science teacher who was leaving the teaching profession after six years in the classroom. It wasn't the students or any problems he had with classroom management, the curriculum, or teacher methods that forced this difficult decision. He had just become overwhelmed with all the extra "hurdles" that his administration and the central office heaped on him. He continually had to jump over these barriers at the end of the day with no extra time to justify grades requiring endless paperwork, make and send three copies of all lesson plans to others within the school system, provide proof of parent contact when he taught over 100 students—the usual things I have been trying to describe to you that take too much time and totally exhaust and frustrate you. The following are excerpts from his article:

> "When a system becomes so deeply flawed that students suffer and good teachers leave (or become jaded), we must examine how and why we do things. Over my six years in education, I've lost my optimism and question a mission I once felt wholly committed to. I still care deeply about students. I've worked hard to brighten their day while giving them an enjoyable and rigorous environment in which to learn. If this job was just about working with students, I

couldn't ask for a better or more meaningful career. The job, though, is about much more. To make a real difference in the lives of students and attract and keep life-changing teachers, we must address five key areas:

1. <u>Tear Down the Hoops</u> Our teachers spend far too much time jumping through hoops. Every year, our district invents new goals, measuring sticks, time-consuming documentation, modified schedules, and evaluations in an attempt to prove we're actually doing something in the classroom, etc. Bad teachers can game any system; good teachers can lose their focus trying to take new requirements seriously. These hoops have distracted me from our priority (students). I've concluded it's no longer possible to do all things well. We need to tear down these hoops and succeed clearly on simple metrics that matter. On a personal level, with 100+ students a year, a growing family, and two side jobs, I can no longer be a good teacher and do all the system expects.

2. <u>Have a Plan for the Future</u> I stepped into the classroom around the time of a major worldwide recession. As the individuals and institutions responsible for this recession escaped accountability for their actions, school districts like ours went into survival mode. Six years later, we're still there. We have no plan for the future. These basic mantras seem to govern what we do: Just do the best you can. We need to do more with less. There's no money in the budget for that. We're hoping things look better next year.

When times are tough, human beings and institutions have the rare opportunity to reflect and refocus, to think differently and creatively. We should have a clear plan for sustainability. Instead, we're really just worried about balancing the budget. When we have a desperate need like football bleachers that have to be replaced, or turf-grass that isn't up to par, we somehow find the money. We—through public or private avenues—meet those needs. Why can't we find funds to address the areas that seem more pertinent to our primary mission?

3. <u>Scrap Obsession with Flawed Assessments</u> I've seen teachers cry over Standards of Learning scores. I've seen students cry over SOL scores. I've seen newspaper and TV reports sensationalize SOL scores. SOL tests are inherently unfair, but we continue to invest countless hours and resources in our quest for our school to score well. This leads me to the following questions: Do we care more about student progress or our appearance? Why can't we start a movement to walk away from these tests? Why can't we shift our focus to critical thinking and relevant educational experiences?

Our new teacher evaluations focus heavily on test scores. But while teachers are continually under pressure to be held accountable, there seems to be very little accountability for parents, the community, or district offices. We have submitted ourselves to these tools that misrepresent student growth. It is a game that I no longer wish to play.

4. <u>Build a Community That Supports Education</u> Stop by the high school for a sporting event (and I love sports) and you'll be impressed with the attendance and enthusiasm. Stop by the high school on a parent-teacher night and you'll

see tumbleweeds blowing through the halls. If parents and local decision-makers really value education (and there is a small portion of the community that does), student and teacher morale would be much different. Our school and political leaders must help build a community that truly supports education. A real investment from residents across all neighborhoods and groups would change the climate immensely and allow us to truly tackle the challenges that lie ahead.

How can we provide high quality education to all students?

How can we build strong academic programs that meet student needs?

How can we prepare students to be productive citizens?

How can we successfully partner with parents and others?

We simply can't move forward when there is such little community connection to our educational goals. And if we can't move forward together, I don't want to tread water alone.

5. Fairly Compensate Educators Compensation alone has not pushed me away from education. At the same time, the years of salary and step freezes have taken a toll. If educators are as valuable as we claim they are, then we would make sure we take care of employees and their families. We must fairly compensate educators. Keeping a sixth year teacher on a first year salary is not looking out

for someone who looks out for students. There's only a $100 difference in my December 2009 and January 2014 monthly paychecks."

Josh Waldron is a current example of the overworked, underpaid, and misunderstood teachers that are there on the line working to educate America's children. He could have written this chapter of our book, which is why I included as many excerpts of his article as I did in this update. His loss is a real blow to the profession because his district, state, and country needs more like him to educate our children. Teachers like Josh need your support, so please get on the education bandwagon and join in to help the results improve. We will all benefit from a united front, because as I said in Chapter III, we are in this together, working to make a good future life for our children possible. Try to understand and become a part of the solution to this never-ending problem of student achievement. In the end, your children will thank you—and so will their teachers.

CHAPTER VI

People (and Sometimes We) Just Don't Understand

"To lead others out of darkness, let them see your light."
—*2 Cor. 4:6 (Paraphrased)*

Voice I:

"It's a Black thing, you wouldn't understand," and "The Blacker the college, the sweeter the knowledge" were popular quotes worn on T-shirts by many of our black students in the late 1980s and early 1990s. Today I say it's a "people thing," and we'd all better try to understand before it's too late.

At that time in our careers, Sue and I would marvel at the boldness of the blacks who proudly wore such clothing. Sue had frequently commented about how whites would be considered racists if they had worn similar statements with the word "White" instead. As a matter of fact, her son, Bryan, considered having such a shirt made, but when Sue suggested that he do it, he reconsidered, saying, "I'd probably get my butt kicked!"

My response back then was that it was just blacks displaying pride in our heritage. After all, blacks had not been able to go to many of the white Ivy League schools and major universities for decades. Traditional black universities, one of which I had attended, enabled black students to obtain higher education when they would have been rejected by other schools because of low SAT or other scores. Although I wasn't brazen enough to buy and wear such a shirt, I felt some pride in the list of schools printed on the backs of the "sweeter the knowledge" shirts because my college, Livingstone College, was listed among them. I further stated to Sue how I felt some whites had displayed racism for years with the wearing of the Confederate flag and the slogan displayed underneath, "The South is gonna rise again." Additionally, when blacks began wearing the X symbol, made popular by Spike Lee's autobiography film about Malcolm X, whites responded with a shirt that read, "You wear your X and I'll wear mine" (the X on this shirt was the symbol of the Confederate flag).

We also commented on the irony of how we had met at Jefferson Davis Middle School, which is now called Davis Middle School in order, I think, to be "politically correct." Years ago the school's band even had grey uniforms reminiscent of the South's Civil War military garb, and their mascot was called, of all things, the Rebel! Believe it or not, this was as recently as the early 1980s, but today Davis proudly displays a colorful and very muscular Bulldog to everyone's delight. Sue was white and from the South (if you consider WV a part of the original VA south), while I was black and from the North. Who could have ever imagined that our very own 20th century version of the Civil War (school can be a battle zone!) would occur in an American classroom where we both would teach and close our ranks to an even playing field by finding success in education.

Despite the civil rights advancements ending segregation and discrimination in public schools, the tension between the races still exists on a large scale, and HEAR THIS WELL: blacks can be racist too. Yes, it is true and it is only when we accept the fact that many of us are, or were, or just have some racist attitudes that the healing can really begin. Again, it is the truth that sets us free. Another truth that I must admit is that I probably had more racist attitudes than Sue did.

Sue is just one of those unique people who takes others for who they are and doesn't judge according to color. She often says, "Color is not a problem—just do what you are supposed to do." However, I still had some bitter feelings toward the white community, but Sue's influence and love helped me move through those feelings and lose long-held resentment. What made our relationship so special was that, despite our differences, we both loved people and shared a desire to pull out the best qualities in our students so they could realize their greater potential. Most importantly, we both loved God and wanted to not only hear and speak His word, but also live it as well.

I once told Sue that it was easy for her not to be bitter or feel hate because she did not have to walk around in a brown package and feel the adverse effects that came from wearing a black "earth suit." However, I did not know that she had family members who had suffered reverse discrimination and acts of "black on white" crime. She called them to task and held them to right saying, "Remember, that this is just some blacks, not all of them," while I thought of the many people I knew who still said, "White people are this," or "Those people are that." That's what I mean—in spite of what happened or happens, Sue won't make excuses for either side. She expects the same from all of us—our best—regardless. So it is no wonder that when I was with Sue out in public, I felt totally at ease. I would laugh with her, hug her, kiss her on the cheek, or pat her back without reservation because I felt free and totally accepted by her. When I was with Sue, I'd forget that racial tension existed. Yet, when I would get the stares from other black females, I was reminded how, I believe, black women seem to have the hardest time coping with mixed relationships.

Many black women were already bitter because some black men still seemed to want white women even after the brutal history of tortures, lynchings, and ridicule experienced in years past by those who dared to speak to, touch, or even look at a white woman. Additionally, black women sometimes felt rejected by their own when black males experienced a high level of success or "finally made it," and chose mates from outside the race as part of the successful image package. Perhaps black women also felt threatened because they rationalized that if white women take "our" men, we may have to consider "theirs" for possible mates. The looks from these women seemed to say, "What is wrong with that sister? Is she also cheating on the race by being friends with a white woman?" The looks only encouraged me to hug Sue a little harder and a little longer. Perhaps they'd get bold enough to ask, and I would be brave enough to say, "This is a God thing, and unless you're one of His, you'll never understand."

Believe it or not, during some of the conversations when Sue and I discussed those bold t-shirt designs, we also discussed and almost argued about that "N" word. Sue's position was "I just don't get it," while I felt that blacks' acceptance of that term among themselves came from the past. During slavery times, whites called Africans "niggers," and the name caught on among the slaves themselves. For example, a house slave who held a higher position on the plantation might refer to a field hand by the term he heard most often used. Today we still use phrases like, "What's up, my nigga" "Nigga, please," or "Nigga, you trippin'" to our closest friends and relatives. It's as if we are saying, "If that's all others can see in me, I'll use and even capitalize from it. I'll use it as if that word can't hurt me."

There was a time that I used it in my family, but as I grew older I realized the detriment I was bringing to myself and other African-Americans and knew I had to stop using that word. Again I say this word is in our history and will continue to perpetuate itself unless exposed and honestly discussed. It reminds me of a young man in an Oprah Winfrey special entitled *The Color of Melanin* who asked why his buddies used that word to refer to each other. "Why don't we say, 'What's up, my friend?' or 'What's up my fine, young African-American?' This was a name given to us by slave masters. Why use it?" It has been said that "children learn what they live," and "we become what we are called." These facts alone should force us to stop using that word. If that is not enough, remember God's word which states, "We are beautifully and wonderfully made." That does not describe a nigger!

Another thing that people just don't understand is that teachers can and do bond with their students in many positive ways. So I want people to realize that after countless days of teaching and interacting with a particular student, you can build a rapport that can last a lifetime. I can still remember the first time I ever experienced the loss of a student. Sue and I both taught him. Emile was a bold and outspoken, but likeable. He was one who had lots of potential, but needed attention and encouragement to overcome some negativity. One Friday he was there; by Monday, he was gone. I remember how I hugged him in the hall on his way to the buses that last day. I told him I was proud of the job he had done in the eighth grade talent show when he had sung, "It's So Hard To Say Goodbye To Yesterday." How ironic his choice of music had been. It was almost as if this song had prophesied his untimely end from a gunshot wound. He died just as the main character, Cochise, did in the 1960 movie *Cooley High* from which the song Emile had sung was taken. The only difference was the movie character was killed in the streets while Emile was found dead at home. They said it was a suicide, but I never accepted that explanation.

Not long after Emile's loss, Sue and I experienced the death of another student—Carlton—who was brutally gunned down in a remote field away from home. I remember how he listed Sue as his favorite "white" teacher and me as his favorite "black" teacher in the yearbook. He was such a good looking and talented kid, and his death was such a waste.

People said he was in the wrong place at the wrong time, but we'll never know.

Years later I lost another student, Albert, to a gunshot wound. He was killed by a home-made gun and died in his father's lap. This was such a waste of a young life.

Finally, there was Devon, who was one of my greatest losses because I had pleaded with the principal to let him come back to school. While suspended, he was killed in a car accident. There were three in the car, but he was the only one killed. It hurt so much because I felt he was one who could have made it, but he slipped through the system. As much as I tried to help him, I couldn't change what happened. Even as I reflect on these losses, it still hurts.

Speaking as a person and as a teacher, I want to try and help people understand all of the things that I have shared in this chapter. My response to everyone is to get over your prejudicial, judgmental attitudes and start trying to understand that we all are people first and races or cultures second! Be willing to open your life to a friend of whatever ethnic group you desire, and move beyond your race, culture, and comfort zone. You don't have to force it; it will come to you naturally. After all, God allows situations to come to us that help us to grow, but the choice to engage will always be ours. I would encourage you to be open to people of other races now, because in Heaven there will be no color lines

Voice II:

After Deidre and I became close friends, we would occasionally go shopping at the mall, check out materials at school supply stores, or eat out at local restaurants. Many times we would see some of our students while we were in these social situations. They usually seemed amused to see the "dynamic duo" together outside the classroom as well as side by side at school. However, we rarely got such a positive reaction from some adults who observed us in the public setting.

People just have to understand that Deidre and I enjoy being together. We laugh a lot as we discuss things that happen at school or with our families, finding humor in most of the situations life throws at us. As we walked through the mall, laughing, joking, and sharing, you couldn't imagine some of the looks we got from people observing our interaction. Black women in particular seemed to be perturbed as they glanced our way. Their rolled eyes seemed to say, "What could those two be so happy about, and why are they shopping together anyway?" We've noticed the looks, the body language, and expressions, but choose to go our merry way, figuring that they just don't get it. They don't understand that our friendship is real and close because we truly care about one another and our families.

I've also had occasion to go out in public with Deidre's husband, Larry. Once when I traveled with the family to Washington, D.C. to support one of the children's activities (I am the Godmother, you know!), Larry and I were the first ones ready to go out the next morning. I went with him to get breakfast for the whole group, and we stopped at both a fast food restaurant and a grocery store before returning to our hotel. At both places, the eyes were checking us out—Larry, younger and black, and me, older and white. We ignored the reactions, not even speaking of it, but Larry later shared with Deidre that he was very aware of people's interest in us at both public places.

These brief experiences have given me some perspective on the challenging situations some people live with permanently because they have chosen to marry someone of a different race. The eyes are always on them, comments made just within earshot, and seemingly constant surveillance from surrounding people in every public situation. Even though such marriages are increasing in number, they are still enough of an oddity that they bring out the curious nature of those who are inclined to stare and gossip. One of my former students who is a fraternal twin from a mixed marriage (black father and white mother) told me that she and her sister are always getting stares when they are out in public with one or both of their parents. One woman was bold (rude?) enough to ask her mother who "those children were she was with?" I don't know how polite a reply I could manage in that situation, especially when it might be the 199th time it has happened. Why don't people understand that we live in a time when some of us are able to see beyond race, color, or culture to love another person. How much better the world would be if more people could live in like manner. Instead of looking for perceived differences, why not embrace our similarities?

I may be white and some people might be quick to say that I "don't understand," but I will never be able to grasp the inequity surrounding the use of the "N" word. I am not inclined to use this unacceptable term for black people which Mr. Webster's dictionary defines as an "ignorant, uneducated person." The definition goes on to say that this word is only acceptable in "black English," a statement with which I do not agree at all. I don't feel it is a term anyone should use. I know if I ever did say this word in public, the disdain of everyone within earshot would be evident unless I was attending a Klan rally! Intelligent white people just don't use that term to describe blacks. It was a name given to slaves and newly-freed men and women over 150 years ago by those who would build themselves up by lowering others through discrimination. I hate that word! It stirs up images of lynchings, cross burnings, and cowardly whites who hid their identities in hooded robes. Why in the world would such a word become a part of

African-American slang, rap lyrics, and movie dialogue? Why is it acceptable for gangsta-style music, young blacks and their white counterparts to greet one another with the phrase, "What's up, my nigga?" I will never get it—how in the world can it be unacceptable for me to use it, but accepted and embraced by your good friend who shares your color? Society as a whole just doesn't understand how divisive this historical, but hurtful word is. In my opinion, a term that divides us instead of uniting us should never be acceptable to anyone.

Another issue that puzzles me is how the public as a whole doesn't understand the uniqueness of the relationships that sometimes develop between a teacher and his/her students. Some students always become closer to you than others, but sometimes circumstances forge a student's face and name into your memory forever. After almost twenty years as a classroom teacher, I can name several memorable students:

There was Sean, the class clown, with gorgeous, curly brown hair, who could easily disrupt a whole class with only a funny look and did so many times during my first year as a teacher.

In that same class was Ira, a troubled underachiever, who couldn't believe that I came to one of his after school basketball games. I met his mother and little sister there in the gym. He was gunned down in the streets and died several years later.

Then a few years later, there was Elton, who had many talents, but also many problems and is now serving a life sentence in prison for a death caused in a drive-by shooting. In my mind, I can still see a beautiful poster he made for a "I Have a Dream" project.

With a tear in my eye, I remember Carlton, an especially precocious and handsome young man, who drove all the girls crazy in the eighth grade. He had an inner, spiritual quality that really drew me to him. I went to one of his Saturday morning football games the year I taught him and met his family, including his mom who was expecting another child that year. After graduation from high school, he was shot and killed in a rural area not too far from our city. Going to the funeral home with Deidre was a very difficult thing to do. It was such a tremendous loss of an incredible young life, and such heartache among so many of his peers. A few years later I would have his sister in my class, the child his mom was carrying when I attended that Saturday morning game years earlier. His family and I had come full circle.

It was Tameka who caused much hysteria and many tears among her female classmates when she left school early to go to the hospital and give birth to her baby on the very day of the eighth grade dance. Her pain upon leaving the building early with other upbeat classmates who were also leaving early to get their hair done for the dance did more to reinforce the concept of birth control or abstinence than any Family Life lecture.

Several years ago it was Charles who was his family's pride and joy. The oldest son, he was a model student who came back to the classroom as a young teacher. I gasped in shock early one morning as I saw his picture in the newspaper, arrested on an assault charge. The disappointment I felt for him and his family was almost unbearable as I reflected on how prominently this article was displayed. It was almost as if the reporter and newspaper took joy in documenting a teacher charged with such an offense. It seems that when a teacher is charged with a crime, "innocent until proven guilty" is rarely assumed.

Finally there was Emile who died during his eighth grade year under suspicious circumstances. He was in my home-base class, one of twenty-eight students. I found out about his death merely by chance after stopping in the neighborhood where flashing lights and police cars seemed to be everywhere. When I asked an officer who was investigating an obvious crime what had happened, he identified the home where he said a young man had died. I went home to check my student info, never thinking that the tragedy could have affected one of my students. But it had and did affect numerous others who couldn't believe that one of their classmates had actually died. That endless week of talking, counseling, crying, and finally speaking at his funeral, was one I will never forget.

Teaching is not just about the curriculum, homework, standardized testing, and report cards. It's also about relationships and memories. The public sometimes doesn't understand how these types of incidences weigh heavy on your shoulders and in your heart. Somehow you have to keep your emotions together, stay strong for your students, and continue to do your job when inside you just want to scream out that life is not fair! For all the wonderful relationships and positive experiences that bring up your spirits as a teacher, there will be those that drag you down and crush you to your core. Believe me, prayer works and sometimes that's all I had to keep me going, but it was enough.

So the next time you drive by your neighborhood school, please remember to whisper a prayer for those inside. The students represent many families, and the teachers and other adults in the building are there doing a difficult job, forming relationships that you may never understand.

TWO VOICES AS ONE…FOR YOU

Of all the things that people don't understand, I guess we want to emphasize the uniqueness of the student/teacher bond. It has been said that "teachers touch the future," but we feel that students definitely touch teachers' hearts. They also have a way of reaching out and teaching us many things in different ways. One of the most important things we can learn from students is how to care and love unconditionally. The best educators anywhere can tell you that students don't really care how much you know until they can tell how much you care. Looking back we realize that some student/teacher relationships continue even after death because we will never forget them.

Although the events mentioned in this chapter are true, student names were changed in order to ensure their protection and privacy.

TEN YEARS LATER

Deidre's Voice:

"It's a Love thing" would be the most important message I would like to echo ten years later or to put it in the frequently used words of my pastor, Bishop McLaughlin, "My color is LOVE." The My Color is Love movement and ministry was actually founded by Pastor Earl Johnson who encourages others to join him. This movement is exactly what Sue and I consistently talk about, and we naturally join his ranks.

As of the update of our book and this particular chapter, I can honestly say that there is so much more happening in society today that I don't even want to begin to understand because our world is so full of evil and anti-Christ attitudes and actions. However, I do understand the times in which we live and that all these events were already prophesied long ago about how evil would prevail throughout our land before the return of Christ. Overall, mankind believes that he is so intelligent due to all of the current inventions and new ways of doing things, but everything will continue to fail as long as people put things and thoughts above God.

Even as I write this chapter, the news is full of critical events taking place daily regarding the insane and corrupt Muslim terrorist group ISIS (ISIL) and how it is causing mass chaos and death throughout Syria and Iraq. It seems as if these dreadful, violent fighters are shouting out to America, "Step across our line or knock this stick off my back if you are really so big and bad!" Additionally, Israel and Hamas are fighting continuously, and God's command for us to pray for the peace of Jerusalem (Israel) looks more futile with each approaching day. To worsen these matters, right in our own backyard, people are rioting in the streets of Ferguson, Missouri, over police brutality and injustices they feel on really personal levels. Still, as these events unfold, others are crying out in so much anger and a total lack of respect for our country's leader who a majority voted into office, but they will not even lift up one voice to pray for this man; a man who obviously lacks a godly back bone and definite morals that demonstrate he is receiving direction from the one true God. Even I now experience regrets over voting President Obama into office. Still, as a Christian I have an obligation unto God to pray for him and for the peace of Israel even when it seems like both situations are hopeless. The sad but true reality of it all is that for the majority of time, our history shows that a leader reflects the people he or she leads. Many do say our president lacks a backbone and tries to straddle the fence on too many widespread issues, including our economy, education, race issues, foreign safety, and policy concerns. Yet, isn't that same malady plaguing the Christian body as a whole? Far too many of us are fence-straddlers. We also lack the backbone and fortitude to step-up and stand-out in America today as the majority voice we as Christians claim to be. It appears that more and more of us are choosing to voice our opinions through complaining to each other instead of praying to the God whom we profess to love, serve, and follow.

In 2004, when our first edition of *Small Voices* was published, there were many topics I had spoken out about with the accompanying "Why?" because I could not comprehend the reason behind it all. Most of the issues about which I pondered dealt with me as an individual person and as a teacher. Today, in 2014, we are truly a global economy and my claim, regards, and problems can no longer reflect just me as an individual. Now, I must view myself as a citizen of the world. My voice, while it is still just one, must now fully engage and be a strong part of the entire Body of Christ because I am His representative on this earth. Therefore, I choose to lend all that I have and am to the cause of Christ.

There may still be so much I choose not to understand or fret about any longer. That is because I have now chosen to fully accept how God is in control. Therefore, it is past the time for all Christians everywhere to rise to the occasion. This occasion is being set in order for us to set aside our own personal agendas because they do not matter. We must seek to find out where we fit into the larger plan. That plan comes from God, and that is what we must seek to understand. As Christians, we must fully understand that our purpose and salvation was predestined for us. If we profess to know God, then love comes with knowing Him because God is LOVE. Thank you, Pastor Johnson and Bishop McLaughlin for promoting what I feel so strongly now more than ever: "MY COLOR IS LOVE!" It just has to be LOVE.

"What color will you **choose** to represent?"

Sue's Voice:

Deidre and I hit a number of diverse topics in our original Chapter VI. Our unlikely meeting in a school which had held too long onto Virginia's Civil War history, the divisions caused by slang and culture, the judgmental attitudes of many people, the precious, sad memories of lives lost too soon, and the impact students can have on their teachers. This chapter is like sitting down with you over a cup of coffee and sharing experiences that impacted us in many ways. Today, I would ask you to share your opinions of what we discussed. For example, are people who automatically judge others because they appear different than what they are used to as much a source of frustration to you as to me? Or do you find yourself in that situation, judging before considering that God loves "those" people too and we are not to judge, but witness to His overwhelming love? I know I do.

Over the past ten years, a lot has changed, but a lot has remained the same—and unfortunately, there seems to be a lot more to judge. So many people of both genders and many ethnicities are using their bodies as a source of artistic expression. Tattoos are not my thing, and sometimes I have to bite my tongue or check my expressions before I become a judgmental example as well when I see this colorful artwork covering entire bodies. Elongated ears filled with mutilating circles, piercings everywhere (don't ask me where I saw the most repulsive one), rainbow hair, etc. can be seen in almost every public setting. That wasn't the norm when Deidre and I first wrote about people observing us and making their verbal and non-verbal criticisms obvious. Now, there seems to be no situation that is unacceptable, and those of us who want to say "No, that's not right," are looked upon as judgmental haters.

For example, more and more couples are choosing to "live together," "shack up," "co-habitate," or whatever you want to call it. God calls it wrong, and it is unacceptable to Him because He designed marriage as a special partnership between one man and one woman, which the Bible explains as mirroring the relationship Christ has with His church. Living with one partner or multiple ones (with "benefits") trivializes and cheapens this special relationship. As a result of these current lifestyle changes, many children are being born to unwed parents. I found a 2013 CBS report stating that 44% of American women give birth by the time they are twenty-five, with only 38% of them being married by that age. The numbers continue to increase as women age because by the age of thirty, 2/3 of women will have had a child out of wedlock. Girls who drop out of high school have their first child at the average age of twenty and don't marry until around age 25. A whopping 83% of first births to non-high school graduates are to unwed mothers. The reason for my mentioning these statistics is the tremendous toll these births take not only on the young women, but also on their offspring, possibly for the rest of his/her life. As a retired educator, this is a real concern for me.

Many researchers and psychologists have documented that children have a better chance at a more stable life and productive future in a home with a mother and father figure. That makes sense because it is the type of family that God designed. Single moms or dads have an incredibly hard job trying to fill both roles.

Divorce is another real concern for me. Sticking it out through tough times seems to be something that doesn't happen too often now days. No marriage is perfect and relationships involving abuse, abandonment, and adultery are Biblically unacceptable. However, tough times require tough people who continue to try their best to fight the bad situations but not each other. In earlier times families stuck it out through the good and bad times making divorce a rare occurrence. However, each generation since the 60s seems to have made it easier to split, and within those splits are children who have no real stability. Many times my sixth graders would come to school on a Monday, dispirited and discouraged because they realized that they had left their book bag at Dad's house and wouldn't be going back until the next Friday. Books, assignments, projects, etc. had been left in another part of town or another city altogether. That's just one example of how broken families, step-parenting, and custody arrangements impact an innocent child. I wish I could solve this problem and make everyone happy within their family grouping because I know the children would fare much better emotionally, and when that happens, they are healthier, happier learners.

I'm not going to say much about same-sex partnerships or marriages. As a Christian I have to stay strong to the core of my beliefs, but I am also responsible for treating others as God would have me to do. That doesn't mean I have to accept their choices, and that doesn't make me a hater as many Liberals would suggest. Acceptance and inclusion are today's buzz words, and our society has been "slowly cooked" for years as was the unsuspecting frog in the pot of cold water that slowly heated until the amphibian was cooked to the point it couldn't escape. I fear by not rejecting things that God says are wrong, we have allowed our society to decay from within. The devil is subtle and slowly allows us to accommodate to changing norms to the point that there is no longer any wrong or right way, just what is most acceptable to most people. It's truly a sad situation.

The bottom line in my discussion of all of these examples is that the classroom is also impacted when children from all kinds of family situations come together to learn. Previous experiences, language choices, mannerisms, dress styles, etc. can clash, and teachers are right in the middle trying to help children understand that we are a learning unit within the classroom first and individuals with differing opinions and lifestyles next. Agreeing to disagree without anger and blame leads to an environment that helps everyone learn and achieve. As a new school year is beginning in my community, I just read a wise posting from Facebook which stated that teachers must model the respect and acceptance of each student for their class to see and copy. I thoroughly agree with this sentiment. Isn't that what we want? Less stress, less arguing, and more acceptance of a person, not necessarily his/her lifestyle. As hard as that may be, remember Jesus taught that we are to "love your neighbor as yourself—love does no harm to its neighbor. Therefore love is the fulfillment of the law." (Romans 13:9-10)

CHAPTER VII

We Agree to Disagree

*"Each man can interpret another's experiences
only by his own."*
—Thoreau

Voice II:

Coming from two very different backgrounds and ages, Deidre and I sometimes disagree on topics in the news or life in general. She will see a totally different scenario than I expected, or I will offer some insight that she hadn't considered. But some topics just seem to have no middle ground, so for the sake of our relationship, we have "agreed to disagree."

Affirmative Action:

As a white, middle class educator, I am all about fairness, hard work resulting in positive rewards, and equal access. However, when I read stories about affirmative action conflicts in the 21st century, I just don't get it! The years since the Civil Rights legislation of the 1960s and beyond should have equaled the playing field for people of color. Why then is it necessary to push for minority hiring, college admittance, etc.? The Supreme Court must have been thinking along those lines when they decided in June, 2003, that the University of Michigan could not assign additional points or use a quota system for African-American students when considering their applications for admittance. In my opinion, affirmative action seems to be a "reverse discrimination" situation or an obvious put-down to African-Americans. It leads to the mind-set that this is the only way people of color can make the grade; that they have to be given advantages because of perceived deficiencies. I don't think this type of backlash thinking was the intention of affirmative action in the first place, and I don't agree that it was meant to be a never-ending program that blacks and others can count on for all time. Not all minorities agree with this system either. The late former NFL football star, minister, and writer, Reggie White, called the affirmative action system "broken," and stated in his book *Broken Promises, Blinded Dreams* that "as long as man looks to man for help instead of looking to his Heavenly Father, he is doomed to fail." African-American editorial columnist, Leonard Pitts, Jr., writes a message to me and others who agree with my way of thinking by saying, "If affirmative action is defined as giving someone an extra boost based on race, white men have always been the biggest beneficiaries of affirmative action since slots for academic admission, bank loans, and public office have routinely been set aside for them over the years." Mr. Pitts goes on to say that "those of us who fail to believe that race is not a significant factor in white success are simply delusional." I might have to disagree with him based on personal experience.

In the early 1990s, I saw how affirmative action affects non-minority students seeking scholarships when my youngest son attempted to qualify for tuition assistance for college. He was told that although his GPA was high and he qualified in other areas, he needed to be a minority to be eligible for the help he sought. Needless to say, that policy and comment left a bad taste in his mouth and gave me a new perspective on government guidelines in this area.

In the business sector, the result of affirmative action type of hiring and supervision has resulted in what I believe to be flawed thinking by company leaders and legal advisors. The unwritten rule that I have observed goes as follows: don't even think about dismissing a black employee, a woman, or other minority without undeniable proof which represents weeks to months of paperwork. It doesn't matter if the person is incompetent, breaks the rules, loses money, comes in late, or has no people skills in dealing with the public or other workers. The perceived reason behind the dismissal or even a temporary suspension will be racism or discrimination. This is the playing card of choice for many in the above categories. Somehow these people do not have the capacity or have never learned to evaluate the reason for the disciplinary action and look within themselves for a problem that needs fixing. The boss is obviously racist or hates women! The sad part of this situation is that the legal representation for many corporations has fallen right in line with this type of thinking. In order to prevent frivolous lawsuits, managers and supervisors are instructed to placate workers and prevent problems by managing these people in such a way as to avoid any conflicts. This unwritten job description is almost impossible to accomplish. The problems continue with more and more co-workers coming to the conclusion that minorities are protected regardless of what they do, but those of the white/male population need not apply for the same treatment. Once again, I just can't understand or approve. I have always felt that each person should be judged by his or her own actions, and held accountable for the same. If people want equal access, then they should play by the same rules. Equality is earned, not given.

Group Identity:

I have lived in an urban area of southern Virginia for over twenty years and have interacted with many races of people in many different settings. Through the years, I have noticed an interesting phenomenon among different groups of African-Americans which I choose to call "Group Identity."

Throughout this book, you may have noticed that Deidre refers to the black race, black women, and black families as "we." I had heard her use this term for years, but as we worked on this book, the reality of the differences between how I viewed my race and the way in which she saw hers became much more vivid to me. I wondered why we viewed people, especially from our own races, differently. I rarely even call members of my own extended family by the pronoun "we," but she includes a whole race of people and uses the term frequently. I guess I'm more of an individualist, rationalizing that in this life, I am only responsible for me, not my brother, my co-worker who looks like me, or the white criminal who ate his victims!

I have also noticed that when I teach the topic of slavery to students as young as eleven or twelve years of age, I hear the same thing from African-American youngsters, "Why did they treat _us_ that way?" "_We_ should have never accepted slavery." These sixth graders personalize this unfortunate part of our history, seeming to really feel a part of it themselves. What happened in the past is remarkably real to them. I guess I could compare it to how some of today's Jewish population view the Holocaust.

Perhaps that is why some African-Americans seem loathe to criticize members of their own race for actions that should easily be viewed as inappropriate, unacceptable, or just wrong. For example, a few years ago, a group of black high school boys were videotaped running through the stands at a football game, beating up on people, and causing a near-riot. To their defense came the Rev. Jesse Jackson, making excuses for what they had done and saying they were only being prosecuted because of their race. It was obvious to anyone viewing the tape that these young men were involved in criminal behavior, yet a man with a religious prefix to his name was there to support them, minimize what they had done, and accuse school officials and the local police of racism. On a lesser scale, I have also seen this type of situation in my community. One black reader in our local newspaper wrote in to protest the printing of pictures of people that had been arrested or were wanted by the police for various crimes because "all you ever print are black people—do you have a racial agenda?" Obviously the paper prints the pictures—black, white, Hispanic, etc.—of people involved or wanted for criminal activity, regardless of race. It's as if some members of the black community are hesitant to accept the facts of a situation and punishment for their own group either because they don't trust the police or officials in charge, or they fear that they will somehow be smeared with the same negative label.

This situation saddens me. I feel that those involved are in need of a healing from the same God that many of these people worship. Each of them has been created in His likeness and is loved by Him. They are not simply part of a group—each is an individual Child of God! Could this Group Identity situation really be a "generational curse" stemming from the history of this nation when blacks needed to stick together to survive because they were all lumped together into the same situation due to color and slavery? I would like to see a true "emancipation" of many African-Americans from the feeling that they are judged because of the misdeeds of others who share their skin tone. I also feel that until the condemnation of the African-American community comes down upon those who are committing the crimes, some blacks will continue to see a charge in the newspaper or a guilty verdict in a court room as racism, not criminal behavior. I would hope that should a member of my own family commit a crime, I would continue to try to support and love the individual, while still holding them accountable for the choices he/she made.

As I look at this issue, I feel we should view ourselves as members of a family, church, or close group, not a race. How can any of us defend bad behavior just because the accused person shares your culture or color? Regardless of who judges you and why, your identity and self-esteem should not suffer from the negative, misguided, perhaps even prejudicial opinions of others. You should be judged for who you are, your positive accomplishments or your negative actions. This type of earthly situation would, I think, be a preview of Heaven because one day a Holy God will do just that!

Voice I:

While I agree with many of the statements that Sue has made, I still feel the need to disagree with some of them. I believe that **Affirmative Action** is necessary. We as a race didn't have the head start that some of our white counterparts had. From the very beginning of our country, it was the whites who were the landowners and heads of financial institutions. Blacks initially had very little, and today we are still left behind. I feel that affirmative action has helped to bridge the gap and has allowed us to make some awesome gains in the last several generations. Some people have truly moved from Harlem into the "Huxtable" lifestyle. However, many of our people are still plagued with the Harlem experience of poverty, drugs, government assistance, and black-on-black crime.

Whites made it a crime for slaves to learn to read, viewing this crime as serious enough to earn the death penalty. Now America is surprised when a majority of blacks consistently score in the lower percentiles of standardized tests. When I taught in a remediation program for over five years, I observed that the majority of our students were black. I believe that this situation does indeed go back to our history when we were not allowed to read.

Many reading these words will feel that I have gone out too far on a tangent. Yet, I feel strongly that if you want to understand a present problem, you must look at the root or history behind it. It is hard for white America to accept the premise that current educational problems affecting black students could actually have stemmed from past injustices. Some people will say:

"Get over slavery—I didn't enslave you."

"Forget Jim Crow because things are equal now."

"You can't use the 'white man is keeping me down' as an excuse anymore because affirmative action has made everyone equal now."

"Blacks have jobs whites can't even get, so get over it!"

To these statements I simply ask how can we get over it when less than five years ago a black man was dragged to death through the streets of Jasper, Texas, and more and more racial profiling has been exposed? Blacks have been and continue to be the target of many injustices because of the past. Jim Crow laws in the South used to prohibit any black man from looking directly at or even walking on the same side of the street as a white woman. Fourteen-year-old Emmett Till was brutally murdered for just whistling at a white woman—it cost him his life! Presently, many black men are still losing their lives of freedom because the jail cells continue to be filled with 80% black males. It seems like once lynching was made illegal, the prisons became the new lynching system for the hated and feared black man.

Over the last five years, more and more racial profiling has been exposed. Because of recent DNA advances, black men convicted of murder, rape, or other crimes have been cleared of their guilty verdicts and freed from prison. Once these men get out of prison, affirmative action laws can work in their favor to help them get an education, secure jobs, and have a better chance at success.

All of these examples relate to the history of African-Americans in this country. History is the past defining the present and perhaps the future. If history is responsible for the Magna Carta, and rights such as having trial by jury and protection of personal property, then why can't history also be responsible for the absence of black role models in the African-American community? Even in life, the laws of nature pretty much dictate that if I start behind, then there's a real strong chance that I will remain behind unless someday something strong, dramatic, or profound is added to put me equal to or at a close second—forget "ahead." Even with such African-American high-profile success stories like Colin Powell, Condoleeza Rice, or Benjamin S. Carson, M.D., for the black community as a whole that someday has yet to happen.

Group Identity:

Sue has noticed and commented that I often refer to African-American people involved in negative incidents as "we." I say that because blacks overall are seen by many as a bad race, just as the color black has often been seen as bad, evil, and disgusting. All you have to do is think about a few negative connotations associated with this color, such as: black lie, black magic, "black balling" someone, blacklist, and a black cat. They all historically symbolize the worst or most evil of all. As a black woman, when I see a black person involved in a negative situation—robbing or killing for little to no gain, or killing each other in street violence over a girl, a pair of shoes, or macho behavior—I feel a sense of failure also. I think, "Look at my people, falling into the same old negative stereotype." I have often said when I hear news reports of a petty crime, "I hope they aren't black." I feel that I am being judged as well because many people judge our race as one. The race as a whole started off lower than others; most were slaves together and likewise, freed together. Even today, I believe strongly the race will either rise or fall together.

Historically, if you were ¼ black, society considered you black. Today, the misdeeds, criminal and negative behavior of 20%-25% of African-Americans color the image of the entire race. It is still hard for us to see ourselves as individuals when we are constantly being reminded of the effects of the past as a whole. In school, students will confront mixed-race peers with the question, "Are you black or white?" Because of preconceived notions, they want to know how to treat this person, based on who they say they are. Halle Berry's white mom is said to have told her daughter, "I am raising you as a black woman because society will make you choose, and treat you as one." That meant she felt she had to rear her daughter as a black woman because she looks black. How sad that in America, you cannot be both black and white—even when you really are. Teachers who have taught mixed-race children probably understand what I mean. Have you ever had students ask for help in filling out the background or personal information on a standardized test because they couldn't find themselves among the list of races?

As long as I have to continue to search for the black faces in whatever is good, right, pure, and the best but seemingly find too few there, I will be disappointed. I have no problem finding them in the newspaper articles, the tabloids, and the crime statistics. As long as that continues, I will be part of the group known as "we" rooting for "us" to make it.

TWO VOICES AS ONE…FOR YOU

Perspective is everything! We can't live another person's life; we can only speak from what we know and have experienced. Understanding and compassion come from communication and close interaction. Deidre and I had to be willing to trust each other enough to reveal our true feelings and open-minded enough to share personal ideas and experiences that helped us both grow. There is no one right answer. Equality truly lies in the "eyes of the beholder." However, in God's eyes, we are all equal and we are all loved!

TEN YEARS LATER

Deidre's Voice:

My pastor, Bishop Vaughn McLaughlin, often tells us that a man's theology is shaped by his morality (or immorality). I totally agree with him in that I accept the one true God, Jesus Christ, and His word as the standard for my belief system and the absolute Truth on any subject. We will only accept, follow, and believe God's word as the final authority based upon our willingness to submit to His will for our lives. People who ask, "Who can really decide who is right?" or "How do you know the Bible is God's word and not man's own interpretation?" are, in my opinion, the same ones who are looking for an excuse to have carte blanche in their lives. Many people want to do as they please with no regards to a higher order or final authority. We can see this in what seems to be the lack of respect for "our" young black men by society as a whole, a situation which upsets and bothers me a great deal. Whenever I think of the brutal shoot-downs of Trayvon Martin (17), Jordan Davis (17), and recently Michael Brown (18), it is as if I had stepped back in time to the days of Emmitt Till when the brutal death of a black male child may have occurred because of perception, beliefs, and life experiences. This reinforces my thinking that this disregard for black males is perpetual and stems from our history. Even in the midst of more chaos occurring ten years later, I must come to a conclusion of truth and reality. As a child of God, I must continue to practice lining up my thoughts with what the word of God teaches us about all matters including what it states about our individual actions. Here is a major statement from the Bible that has been translated into plain words from *The Message* (MSG) version for us to ponder:

"Don't be misled: No one makes a fool of God. What a person plants, he will harvest. The person who plants selfishness, ignoring the needs of others, ignores God, and harvests a crop of weeds. All he'll have to show for his life is weeds! But the one who plants in response to God, letting God's Spirit do the work in him harvests a crop of real life eternal life."—Galatians 6:7-8

Read it in whatever translation you like. The truth remains that we will be held accountable for our own actions one way or another. Nobody will get "away" with doing wrong whether we believe that or not.

We all have an opinion. Most of the time our opinions are wrong or greatly askewed based on a variety of factors including our backgrounds, what we are taught as children (laws of first truths), our experiences, and now subjective relativism (doing/believing what is right in one's own eyes). Therefore, in our natural minds, we will find it necessary to continue "to agree to disagree." Perhaps this will help relieve tensions in our minds, feelings, and perceptions. Yet, my spiritual mind, that is the mind of Christ that I must allow to rule within me, agrees with God's word where it states in Judges 17:6, "In those days there was no king in Israel, but every man did that which was right in his own eyes." (KJV) How profound and prophetic that statement written over twenty-two hundred years ago is because I can easily make that applicable right now and say, "In our current day, there is not one acceptable standard in America; so that every person can go about doing what he or she wants to, and feel real good doing IT because 'right' and 'wrong' have no definite meanings anymore." Furthermore, we are being fed a tremendous lie that there is a "new normal" now. It is obvious that when it comes down to doing what is right, our morals and beliefs do shape our theology for good or bad.

This means that we are now being forced to choose sides and take a stand, and I firmly take my stand on the Lord's side.

Whose side are you on and where are you standing?

Sue's Voice:

After the last few weeks, I feel as though I have revisited this chapter and definitely the next one. It's an ironic coincidence that we have come to rewrite our thoughts and feelings on this chapter at this time . . . or is it? Events in Ferguson, Missouri, have reared their ugly head, as a policeman has killed Michael Brown, reminding me of the Trayvon Martin/George Zimmerman case several years ago in Florida. Knowing someone's name by memory is never a good thing because the story or moral learned is rarely a good one. I have many "friends" on Facebook, and some of them are from my teaching career in another state. A large majority of these friends are African-American and the opinions/statements I have been reading have saddened me greatly. Are we really STILL so divided by race in this country? Can we not have some common ground when events like this occur? Couldn't our positive interactions within our belief in God and our shared professions help bring us somewhat together? Once again it seems like history and perspective rule when a national news story can cause such disruption and distance between those who are white and those who are not. I want to speak out and share opinions, but hesitate, knowing that my words will be misconstrued and evaluated due to my skin color and perceived background. We need a heavenly mediator to heal the underlying wounds in our country, or we are only another incident away from riots, destruction, and further division once again. I so long to see all of us move forward together— won't you join me?

CHAPTER VIII

Must We Repeat History?

"Those who do not learn from the past,
are destined to repeat it."
—George Santayana

Voice I:

Through the years, I have gone out to minister in various correctional facilities, and I even helped pioneer the first Marine Institute on Virginia's peninsula. This was a program that used nautical concepts and knowledge, along with marine life, in a final attempt to catch troubled and delinquent youth before they were put through the criminal justice system. Needless to say, at both types of facilities, the majority of the faces were male. I can't even begin to count the number of times I left a jail cell feeling such emptiness, sadness, and depression because the majority of the male faces I saw there were black like mine. "Black like mine" echoed in the far recesses of my mind, and it never left. I often asked myself "why." I even asked God "why." His revelation came to me from the greatest and wisest book ever written—the Bible. Even though many great psychiatrists have stated that the way to solve a problem is to search for its roots, the Bible taught this concept even earlier: "Ye shall know the truth, and the truth shall make you free" (John 8:32). The Bible is our greatest resource and reveals to us that our past can influence our present and our future. As I studied these words, God revealed to me the answer to my question.

The history of black men in our country involves one of much shame, defeat, separation from home and family, as well as antagonizing and ridicule by many of the majority white males. I was shown that the result of this treatment and other factors over the years have left many black men torn down and unlikely to become assets in our society. In reality, I see a large number of black men being a liability. Not only are they liabilities in prisons, but are being seen as such on the street corner—hanging out, selling drugs, and leaving yet another legacy of wasted lives.

When I asked where are our forefathers, our brothers, our daddies, and our sons when communities were being forged, developed, and founded, the answer came that our men were being brutalized, beaten, downtrodden, and bred like animals from plantation to plantation. They were also scorned in open shame and hung out like pieces of meat, burned the stake, and left out for all to see. Out of this past came fear, shame, anger, and hurt. While the majority of white men had many advantages, the majority of black men had little to nothing. When blacks did try to achieve, they were sometimes brutally reminded to "stay in their place." The past definitely influenced the future as described in Exodus 20:5: "Punishment for the sins of the fathers shall be visited on the child to the third and fourth generations," meaning the negative attitudes, low self-esteem, and apathy, like sin, are perpetual and have been passed down from the father to the son. While many blacks overcame obstacles, remained strong and proud, becoming as successful as possible for their time and circumstances, others continued the negative attitudes that would hurt the black community. Like mold on bread, the spoil ruins the fresh, or one bad apple spreads its rot to the whole bushel.

Thank God for the kind white people He positioned to risk their own lives and families to treat blacks as equal and decent human beings. They gave some of our people land, homes, and hope. This hope was given to an otherwise doomed people. Even with these unselfish acts of kindness by some whites, the majority of black men would still live on to perpetuate separation, despair, and defeat within the walls of the black communities. Additionally, like every race of people, we have lost a portion of our men to homosexuality, interracial marriages, and prison. For the black community, these latter things have proven detrimental to our security and growth. With so many of the black men dead, despondent, or defeated, the black women were left to rear the children who would become the next generation.

My experience has shown me that a majority of discipline problems in the schools in my area have truly been with young, black males. Why? I feel it is because in public schools, you have a majority of black and white women trying to teach and discipline our black males, and this is a very difficult task. As I mentioned earlier (Ch. III—Teacher to Parent), it takes a man to make a man, as well as consistently maintain behavior in the classroom. These boys only respect power, viewing power from a male perspective, and may not initially respect a female teacher. While some female teachers succeed in this situation, many women have an uphill battle to gain respect from certain black males, and chaos in the classroom can result. Many black male students have been reared in homes where Mom is the only working adult. Our black community also contains many successful two-parent families, but I am focusing on those situations that continue to breed poverty, educational failure, and the defeated mindset that says, "I need my check from the government to survive."

Many of our black youth see the only way out of poverty as sports, rap music, or drugs. Why is it when I asked a group of fourth grade students what their future goals were, all of the black boys told me they wanted to go into the NBA or NFL? Why didn't the idea of medicine, law, scientific research, or the military enter their minds? Likewise, when I substituted for a group of high school students, all of the black males came into the room in a disruptive manner, gravitated to the back of the room, started playing cards, and refused to participate in the day's assignment. They refused to see school as relevant and the key to their future. While these two groups might represent only a small portion of students out there, they show that this way of thinking still exists and will continue to affect many on a wide scale. We must work to change these mindsets because I believe overall that the black community still does not see ourselves as college graduates, business owners, or financially free. This is the legacy of the past, and it must end now because negative thinking has hurt us drastically.

I believe now more than ever that all people hurting over past and present injustices need to allow God to heal and change their hearts and minds. Once, when I was sharing my negative feelings about the "white man's" role in the destruction of the black community, a friend, Pastor Butler, sharply reminded me how God had nailed all excuses to the cross. She went on to say that blacks as well as all other races of people must choose to rise above hate, prejudices, and injustices by emphatically stating, "Either you believe God's word or you don't!" This conversation reminded me that Sue had also told me about Reggie White, the famous late former NFL player, speaking similar words in a recent book (see Ch. VII). I thought about all of this and came to the conclusion that since I am a child of God, I had to believe that she and Reggie White were absolutely right. Just like Sue, Pastor Butler provided more healing to my wounds. Still I pondered, "Then how do we help the non-believers or people with no hope, no purpose, or knowledge of God's plan for their lives to overcome and change their negative mindsets?" I believe that these people can only benefit from our prayers for them and our lifestyles before them as children of the Light. Those of us who believe in God are His mouth-pieces and truly are the small voices of people in the middle (see Ch. XII) who will continue to make a positive difference to others around us. We can effectively do this by becoming our best for service to others first and ourselves last. Conclusively, I have chosen to believe that because God delivered the Jews, the slaves, and the Gentiles, that He can deliver us all.

Voice II:

I grew up during the Civil Rights movement. During my junior high years, Martin L. King, Jr. was marching, and students were staging sit-ins and riding interstate buses into the dangerous South to register blacks to vote. I remember being absolutely infuriated when George Wallace stood blocking the doorway of the University of Alabama to the entrance of black students. In West Virginia I knew very few black people, but even at that young age, I realized that what was happening before the television cameras (and before Forrest Gump memorialized it in theaters) was very, very wrong. I wrote Gov. Wallace a letter in bright red ink for emphasis, and told him, "You are a redneck who embarrasses people like me who look like you!" When I mailed the letter, I felt that I had done my part for the Civil Rights Movement.

During my years as an Air Force wife, I would occasionally meet spouses who represented different racial groups, but I never became friends with any of them, nor invited them to our home. However, I do remember an incident in Biloxi, Mississippi, when our oldest son entered the second grade at Jefferson Davis Elementary School. Picking him up after his first day at this new school, my husband and I were eager to hear all the details of his experiences. The one thing that seemed to interest Ric the most, but also appeared to cause him some concern, was the fact that his new teacher, Mrs. Nixon, was black. She had seemed exceptionally sweet and understanding when I dropped him off that morning, but now Dad was going into the school in uniform to pick up our son. As Ric climbed into our van, he nervously turned to his father and asked, "Did you see my teacher? She's black, you know." Richard and I grinned, thinking this was certainly an obvious observation. However, looking back I realize that since our family had not had any close interaction with black people, Ric had no experience with them. I'm glad his first such relationship was with a positive, caring, and professional woman. I'm also thankful that Dad didn't disappoint our son by having a negative reaction to this new learning environment. Imagine the difference it would have made if he had not accepted a black teacher for his son or had made comments criticizing her race. This is how it all starts and racial discrimination infects another generation. I am reminded of the lyrics of the song, "Carefully Taught" from the musical, *South Pacific,* which states in part:

> "You've got to be taught before it's too late, before you're six, or seven, or eight, to hate all the people your relatives hate, you've got to be carefully taught."

Must we repeat history, or can we as American citizens agree that the past is gone, and that we will learn from it and move on? If not, the result may be similar to that occurring elsewhere around the world. Arabs and Jews call the same patriarch "Father" because Abraham sired both Ishmael and Isaac. His descendants are now warring with each other, causing death and destruction in the Middle East. In Northern Ireland, Catholics and Protestants have a long history of religious bigotry and bloodshed. In Africa, tribal warfare has caused massacres of hundreds of thousands of people. Let us learn that this type of behavior is the bitter fruit of hatred and discrimination. America should be better than that because it was founded on Judeo/Christian principles. We could become the country that is described on the base of the Statue of Liberty* if only we decide to look Above for the answer. Every generation has its defining moment. I hope this is ours—that we look to the One who created us all and realize that we are all children of the same Heavenly Father. One of His greatest commandments asks us to love others as we love ourselves. Will we finally get it right? I hope so.

* "Give me your tired, your poor,
Your huddled masses yearning to breathe free,
The wretched refuse of your teaming shore.
Send these, the homeless, tempest-tossed to me,
I lift my lamp beside the golden door!"
—Emma Lazarus

TWO VOICES AS ONE...FOR YOU

It is time for the past to be put to rest, especially in the areas mentioned in this chapter. Personal perspective can be a powerful thing for when a person has had one negative experience after another, he/she sometimes feels that his/her life will never change. As teachers, we are all about change and the transformation that education can bring into a person's life. History that is shameful and wrong never needs to be repeated. It is our hope that this chapter will help at least one person decide that the future is the place to reside. Preparing for and looking to the future gives all of us hope that tomorrow will be much better than today.

"If history repeats itself, and the unexpected always happens,
how incapable must man be of learning from experience."
—George Bernard Shaw

TEN YEARS LATER

Sue's Voice:

Over the years of my teaching career, I taught language arts, reading, and a little math before deciding that social studies was my subject of choice. Sitting in my classrooms were sixth and eighth graders learning about U. S. History, Ancient World Civilizations, and Civics & Economics. The teacher learned right along with the students more than she was ever taught in her high school and college classes, since the best way to truly learn a concept is to teach it. Overwhelmingly, the lesson learned in the history and civilization classes was that human beings don't change much and never seem to learn from the past mistakes of earlier peoples; hence, the title and quote of our original Chapter VIII.

Today happenings from around the world break my heart as innocents are slaughtered in the name of religion (shades of the Crusades), people disrespect and hurt one another on a daily basis, and national and local news stories focus on the negative because there is so much of it! I know there are positive things happening locally and globally because I am connected with some of it, but overwhelmingly the world is in bad shape with many people questioning whether we are living in the End Times predicted by the Bible. In reviewing the warnings for these times, I found the following listed:

Wars and rumors of wars: *"For nation will rise against nation, and kingdom against kingdom and in places there will be famines and earthquakes."* Matthew 24:7. This verse describes what we see and hear reported daily in the news media. The development of weapons of mass destruction and the threat of terrorism are spreading throughout the world. Although most people I know are blessed to have all they need, there are those in my community and across the United States that are living in or on the brink of poverty. Pictures of starving children in third world nations or those in our own country living in terrible conditions are so upsetting to see. The unpredictable weather throughout the world only adds to the loss of crops and the food supply, and I have never heard of so many earthquakes, tornadoes and even a tsunami affecting our world.

Tribulation: *"But all these things are merely the beginning of birth pangs. Then they will deliver you to tribulation, and will kill you, and you will be hated by all nations on account of my name."* Matt. 24:8-9. As I write I am listening to the continuing account of Isis moving across the Middle East, torturing and slaughtering women, children, and other innocents, simply because they are Christian. These people fled their homes, leaving all their possessions behind in an attempt to save themselves and their families. Similar persecution has happened in Africa for years with tales of Christian children for sale in marketplaces right along with salt and other items. While Christians may worship as they please in many countries without discrimination, those in China, Saudi Arabia, Sudan, Russia, and North Korea, to name a few, can suffer persecution and even death for doing so. Sometimes the attack is more subtle—it may come through social rejection, the court system, the school system, or in the work place, but it's here and spreading. I heard a Creation Physicist say during a presentation recently that they need more Christians in the science field now because in the future you may not be allowed to enter that field of study if you are a Christian and don't believe in evolution. It doesn't seem possible that this is happening in America in 2014! But it was predicted long ago.

One-World Government: As predicted in Daniel, Revelation and other Biblical books, we now have the global media, communications technology, and transportation methods that are necessary to allow this to happen. Unity has happened among European nations, even to issuing a common currency, so this prediction is not hard to imagine.

Increase in Knowledge: *"But as for you, Daniel, conceal these words and seal up the book until the end of time; many will go back and forth, and knowledge will increase."* Daniel 12:4. We are living in an era where anyone can find answers to almost any question. The explosion of knowledge that has occurred in the last generation is almost unbelievable. Through the internet we can be and see almost anywhere through applications like Facetime, live cams, and Skype. News from around the world is instantly transmittable through network television. For those who couldn't understand how everyone on Earth could know that Jesus has returned as predicted . . . think about it. It's possible now.

The Return of Jews to Israel: *"I will bring you from the nations, and gather you from the countries where you have been scattered with a mighty hand and an outstretched arm and with outpoured wrath."* Ezekiel 20:34. *"In that day the Lord will reach out His hand a second time to reclaim the remnant that is left of His people . . . He will raise a banner for the nations and gather the exiles of Israel . . . from the four corners of the world."* Isaiah 11:11-12.

As of May, 1948, this condition has been met. Israel was established, and Jewish people from around the world continue to settle there. This is their homeland—the land given to their ancestral father, Abraham, ages ago. I'll leave the conclusions about the End Times up to you, but the facts listed above really give me a reason to "keep looking up."

On our homefront, the stories circulating on social media and reported in the news mirror the mistakes of the past and make me wonder if we will ever get it right in the area of relationships with others. We are in a "hurry up" society and have no patience with those at the check-out counter, the drive-through window, or in the other lane of traffic. As I mentioned in the previous chapter, racial relations do not seem to be improving with both sides distrusting and judging each other. With tens of thousands of undocumented people crossing our southern borders, there are many more people speaking a language other than English and bringing their cultures into America. We have to work together to make this country succeed at a higher level. Suspicion, resentment, and distrust do not lead to that kind of cooperation. Many people don't even trust law enforcement officers any more due to publicized police brutality incidents. That is a step back, and I want us to move forward.

As a mother and retired teacher, I want this world a good one for our children. If we don't learn from past mistakes, their environment will be less than ideal. Those trusting innocents deserve better from us. Children were not born with prejudice, judgmental attitudes, or violent tendencies. They learned it at home, in the school setting, or from films and video games—just from life itself. We need to do better.

Deidre's Voice:

Must we repeat history? Unequivocally, yes, is the obvious answer. No one has to look far to notice that major events that have plagued our nation and the world in the past continue to be repeated on a much larger scale as the days unfold. The Bible does indeed predict and depict these dire events for us to use as signs of the end-of-time. Christians need not have our eyes closed or be blinded by the cares of this world because God is sending us warnings to get our business and life affairs in order before He cracks open the sky.

Sue does an awesome job of lining up scripture with some of the current events and I agree with everything she states within her TYL (Ten Years Later) message for this chapter. I would like to add that based on these Biblical prophesies, it is time for God's people to focus on our purpose. We need to know and do our part in getting the Gospel out to a lost and dying world. We must lose our focus on "things & stuff" and choose God wholeheartedly. We need to ask for a heart of compassion, love, and a true burden for lost souls. Our focus must be on the ministry of Christ as we help present the Truth to all people. We must share about the blood of the Lamb who died once for all, and we must tell our testimony to help as many people as possible within our sphere of influence and community come to the realization that Jesus is Lord, and why they need to accept Him as their Lord and Savior!

Because we are so global now, the international news continues to give us opportunities to hear, see, know, and perhaps understand the world events unfolding each day. It is up to us to discern truths from facts through the lens of God's word and draw our own conclusions on what is being presented to us as truth and reality. Many times while information is being presented as facts, some of it is slanted, biased, or full of someone else's opinions that may not even have a clue about God or the Bible. News may also be distorted depending on what station you watch. There are so many to choose from, but I now circulate and watch three major stations during one setting in order to help give me a more balanced view. I also practice praying for God's help and direction in all matters.

Must we repeat history? Why yes. In fact the biggest repeat of history is taking place right now over the use of the name JESUS! In Acts 4:5 6, Peter and John were being held in prison by the Sanhedrin or main leaders because they did not want them to speak about the resurrection of Jesus or tell the testimony of how the healing of the man by the pool was accomplished, "In the name of Jesus!" Today, we cannot say Jesus in a public arena during an open or general type of prayer.

Many times, we are not even allowed to pray. We cannot say the name of Jesus on TV, in school, or even after school unless it is done in a discreet manner or has gone through several levels of approval by different leaders just like what the first church had to endure. One recent report told how a football coach was put on suspension for praying with his team and using the name of Jesus. Military chaplains are restrained by commands not to pray in Jesus' name when they minister to our service personnel. Also, my pastor told us how he was asked to pray at a major event in our large city, but also asked not to end it with, "In the name of Jesus."

People, if you don't believe history is repeating itself, you need to wake up from underneath that rock hovering over you. Many are dying for the Faith right now in other countries for situations that we still take for granted like having a choice in our place of worship, carrying our own Bible in public, or openly professing Christianity.

In the history of Christianity, the first church of believers in Christ were the most hated group of people who were mistreated, burned at the stake, crucified, fed to lions, and stoned to death. Will we also repeat history and have to die for what we believe? It could happen. In order for the first church to be established, many had to die as martyrs for the cause. Even when Jesus was born, death was connected to Him and His name, as many children under the age of two were massacred by King Herod who feared a new king's birth that was told to him by the three kings from the Orient. In the historical period when the Romans ruled, many people worshipped idols and served many gods. Their lifestyle included men sleeping with men, animals, and women other than their wives. The people of God, known as the Jews were the least regarded inhabitants because they were foolish enough to serve their One God. Out of this group of Jews would be born an even less popular group known as Christians who dared to believe that God had come to earth, died, was buried, and rose again for the entire sins of mankind. Even though signs and wonders followed the disciples of Christ, they were still told to be silent or else they were put to death. Both historians and scholars report evidence on how most apostles and many other Christians died untimely, horrific deaths for maintaining their beliefs in Christ.

Therefore, many—even most in the last church who are alive before the imminent return of Christ—may also have to die for His sake. That same purpose will be fulfilled more and more as Christians right here in America will have to take a firm stand against our government and the spirit of the anti-Christ, while we refuse to denounce the ministry and the name of Jesus Christ on any level. In the global economy in which we live, America's turn to "ante up" is coming. Some of us right here in our own country may have to die for using the name of Christ because I believe history, has, does, and will continue to repeat itself until He returns.

Just think about how much attitudes towards Christians have changed as Christianity has transitioned from powerful to pitiful over the decades. More importantly, through each era of change, you still find remnants of proof regarding how history does, in fact, repeat itself.

In the 1950s, Christianity was still popular and socially acceptable. During that era, people would clearly and willingly define right and wrong. The church leaders preached Jesus and hell's fire without fail, similar to the fervor of the First church.

As the 60s and 70s came on the scene, many people began to ignore the teachings of the Bible and a faithful Christian life-style as the Baby-Boomers became young adults and began to band together as they promoted free sex, free love, free food, free expression in the arts, and peace with your brother as you smoked marijuana and tried LSD together. Some church leaders and Christian parents watched those bold youths rebel, hoping it was just a phase they would outgrow. Some did; some didn't, but Christianity had been changed tremendously.

During the 80s and 90s, Christianity reaped the carry-over from that selfish earlier spirit as church leaders tried to pull people back into the church and began to promote prosperity by faith messages like "Speak it/be it; name it/claim it and touch it/own it." Christians were losing the battle on distinguishing themselves from others as they pursued material gain for their families. Some Christians lost perspective on being responsible to God and His word, and the divorce rate in the church equaled, and then exceeded, that of non-Christians. Children from Christian families were no longer attending church, mainly because their parents stopped going on Sunday due to the exhaustion of working overtime to afford the two cars (for the two-car garage), TV's in every bedroom and the family room, and all the other comfort and status symbols. The term "latch-key" child was coined as many children came home to an empty house without any or very little parental supervision since two incomes were now necessary to afford the chosen lifestyle. As the divorce rate soared, more homes became one-parent ones led mostly by women. It was a new type of national warfare claiming the men—the God-ordained head of the home. This was no Pearl Harbor, and while it was a different type of war, satan's attack on the family appeared as sudden and unexpected as the one in 1941. The casualty count was high, and the institution of marriage was shaken to its core as man took his eyes off God and began focusing on idols. It appeared to be sudden and unexpected; just like the deadly Japanese kamikaze attacks, the feminist movement led its own type of suicide.

As many of these individual partakers brought about her own demise, she also killed off others who may have been closest to her. As more women began to leave their homes in pursuit of doing "their own thing," there were more latch-key children, more extra-marital affairs, more pursuit of "things & stuff," and less pursuit of God. Women who did not need to leave their homes due to circumstances or cultural differences, chose to leave until the major role and purpose of women in a lot of homes was killed off from within. All of these attacks were spiritual and fatal.

Meanwhile, church became a place for pageants and social gatherings as the world watched and began to hate Christians for claiming to be Christ-like while acting more and more like the world. The TV and news media began to consistently berate church leaders because of their financial greed, sexual affairs, debauchery and numerous other scandals. As a new millennium approached, technology began to take the place of face-to-face communication, and door-to-door evangelism took a huge back seat to computer time.

Must we repeat history? Of course we must due to the hardened hearts of men. Now as the year 2015 approaches, people want to serve God on their own terms—mainly from home via satellite TV or the internet or not at all. The idols are now cell phones, I-pods, TV shows/movies on-demand TV, Red-box, Hollywood personalities, Facebook, Twitter, Instagram, and virtual reality games to name just some of the gods of the 21st century. Now more than ever, believers who try their best to live by the Bible teachings of Jesus Christ are being frowned upon, disliked, mistrusted, and seen as a narrow-minded, antiquated, out-of-touch-with-reality group of people.

Professing Christians are once again the minority in a culture surrounded by sexual perversion, slavery, divorce, and fantasy/ecstasy drugs. Men are still sleeping with men; so the women are now sleeping with women, and every type of sexual situation is being made "legal" by man's standards. For instance, two men or two women can never really boast about how they are married. The most they can realistically claim to have is a legal union. Man cannot take a God-ordained and God-defined institution like marriage and try to put his own terms to it. It will only end in disaster. Follow my thinking: scientists have clearly defined terms for everything including a tornado, hurricane, tsunami, earthquake, or even something as simple as a cumulus cloud. Each one of those acts of nature has different aspects or qualities depending on how they operate. If I were to call a tornado an earthquake, I would quickly be corrected by most or considered a fool if I did not comply with the acceptable standard definition. Marriage is no different; only a fool can believe him or herself to be in a marriage if it is not done according to God's meaning, purpose, and definition. The reason why history keeps repeating itself and couples keep failing where marriage is concerned is because people want to remain in a marriage without God. How do you play a basketball game without a basketball, court, and baskets? You don't! Just go ahead and try to play this game with a football—you will fail every time. People will continue to repeat history and fail at marriage as long as they attempt to do it without God.

Must we repeat history? Yes! As long as man chooses to live this life outside of recognizing God, he will continue to fail. He must call on the one true God as sovereign and stop serving other gods. There is only one God who we all should and must serve in order to complete our purpose on this earth.

Must we repeat history? If you believe the answer to that question is "Yes," then ask yourself, "Even if it comes down to my death, would I be willing to be a martyr for Christ?" I believe I would, but I am still working on that one by asking God to prepare me to be ready just in case I am chosen to be a Stephen, a Paul or a Peter in these evil and last days. I want to know from God's revelation to me that I mean it when I say, "For God I live, and for God I will die!"

CHAPTER IX

The Reality of Race: Operation Oreo

"If you can learn a simple trick, Scout, you'll get along a lot better with all kinds of folks. You never really understand a person until you consider things from his point of view . . . until you climb into his skin and walk around in it."
—*To Kill A Mockingbird, Harper Lee*

Voice II:

Our urban area of Hampton, Virginia is culturally and ethnically diverse, and this diversity is represented in the schools as well. My sixth and eighth grade classrooms might contain a 40%-45% Caucasian, 40-45% African-American, and 10%-20% mix of Asian, Hispanic, and mixed-race students. This "melting pot" made for a wonderful eclectic academic atmosphere, but could also cause negative clashes and misunderstandings at times. One of the points I tried to emphasize in as many ways as I could was that you cannot judge a person based their "earth suit," their skin color; that the way people looked was not a determinate of what kind of person they were. I tried to teach my students that what mattered most was the kind of person they were on the inside—that their character, their soul was much more important. My friendship with Mrs. Hester was evident to all our students, and occasionally we would team-teach on a topic or project of interest to us both. One of the most unique of these projects would come to be known as "Operation Oreo."

Part of the opening each day in my social studies classes is to have a discussion on current events—the news. For a long time this particular year, one of the leading stories concerned the O. J. Simpson murder trial. I tried not to dwell on this brutal case, but would relate important developments as they occurred. Finally, the verdict was about to be announced and was scheduled for 1:00 p.m. on a weekday when the third period class would be in my room. Since I had a television set—affectionately called "Big Bertha"—attached to cable and permanently set up in a corner of my room since it would not fit in the library storage room, several adults also found their way into my class that day so they could hear the verdict also. Everyone was quiet as Judge Ito read the jury's verdict: "**N**ot **G**uilty." Almost immediately the room became loud with cheers and clapping, and as I looked toward the noise, I was struck with a sight I will never forget. Most of my black students were joyously expressing their pleasure with the verdict, while many of my white students were incredulously looking on in amazement, their mouths dropping open.

The principal and assistant principal looked on with me, and we all remarked later on the racial divide that was evident in my room that day. How could the same group of students hear the same news reports, analyze the same data, and be so overwhelmingly divided as to the fairness or rightness of the verdict? I came to the conclusion that it was all a matter of cultural perspective. The black students felt that O. J. got a fair trial, and that he was acquitted because no one proved he had committed the crime. Finally, the "black man" had gotten justice and fair treatment in a court of law. The white students seemed to feel the exact opposite; that the trial had proven this man guilty beyond a reasonable doubt and that there had not been justice, but injustice done that day by the jury.

The next day when I walked another class to the cafeteria for lunch, I once again noticed a phenomenon that had interested me earlier in the school year but "screamed out" at me this day. Upon looking around the crowded cafeteria, it was obvious that racial segregation was occurring. Not the illegal kind, but a self-imposed preferential kind. The students were almost entirely sitting with people who looked like them. Black students were sitting together, as were white ones. The Asian, Hispanic, and other students had also chosen to eat with and talk to those of their own ethnic background as much as possible. I decided to try an experiment to bridge this cultural divide with not only this class, but my other three classes as well.

I described the scenario I had witnessed to my third period class the next day and asked them questions about each other. Did Tommy know where Makalia had gone to elementary school? Did Jamal know whether Billy or Susan had any brothers? What was Angela's favorite food? When the lack of answers proved puzzling to the class, I announced a week-long experiment. These students were to regroup themselves during lunch and sit beside someone from their class that they did not really know, someone who did not look like them. During their lunch time that next week, they were to share information about themselves with this classmate and get to know one another in a new and more personal way.

When I went to the cafeteria on the first day of "Oreo" week, there they were, regrouped, and talking away! When they saw me, they waved, wanting me to see that they were doing what I had asked. By Wednesday, these new groups were interacting as if they had been doing this for a long time. I walked over to the tables, and the groups got noisier. I told them that I was proud of them and asked how it was going. They started chanting, "Oreo, Oreo," and began putting their hands in the middle of the table, alternating colors—one white hand, one black hand, etc. The principal saw and heard all the commotion at the table and because several of the larger students were bent over the middle of the table to stretch in their hands, she was concerned that something serious was happening. When I explained to her what we were doing, she was on board with it immediately, and we both reached in and put our hands in an appropriate spot. We were honorary members of the Oreo Society. Both of us felt that this was a dynamic moment. How different from the previous week when students were not united, but divided by perceived differences.

Later, when we discussed what the students had learned during this experiment, what I had hoped would happen had, indeed, occurred. Students learned that they were much more alike than different. Little brothers were a pain, regardless of whether they were black, white, Asian, or Hispanic. Everyone was interested in music, clothes, movies, makeup, etc. They were all teenagers and had a lot of things in common, but they had never taken the time to really get to know people who looked differently than they did. We took that topic to a world view, and decided that people in South America, Africa, Asia, Europe, and Australia would probably have some of the same similarities that Americans do. Eighth graders were able to come to the conclusion that our most important similarity is our humanity—we are all more alike than we are different. What a blessing to see that what I had innately felt all my life and learned personally from my friendship with Deidre had been multiplied into many more lives.

Voice 1:

Like Sue, I noticed the racial divide, but unlike the response she had, which was to find a way to teach or incorporate a life lesson, I needed to internalize it more—analyze why it was so. I pondered over what I had seen and heard repeated about O. J., until I just stopped watching everything about the case on TV. This was a month prior to the verdict, and I began asking myself and God, "Who else would have wanted Nicole dead?" Each day I prayed that God would allow this vicious killer to be found. What person would commit such a hideous, unspeakable crime and take a mommy from her precious babies?

Who would do such a thing? My mind continued to come to the same conclusion—it had to be O. J.! He probably did it or had someone else do it. When an answer from God didn't seem to come, my mind still told me, "The Juice did it!"

It amazed me that I didn't feel angry that this man I thought was guilty had been set free from this terrible crime. Honestly, a part of me felt relieved or justified. I further rationalized that a lot of blacks probably felt that O. J. was guilty, but for once a black man had enough money and enough reputation to buy his freedom. The wicked spirit of buying indulgences (a Catholic term which meant paying for sins) was now affecting a new race and era. Still another part of me was glad. Now white America could see how so many blacks felt when the guilty, smug murderers of Emmett Till were declared not guilty, or when four precious, innocent church girls were killed by the Klan in Birmingham, Alabama. I was so torn by my feelings because in reality, this verdict had nothing to do with earlier times. I could only ask God to forgive me for how I felt. It was wrong for me to rationalize that what was done so long ago could justify why a part of me was satisfied that O. J. was found not guilty. That was wrong, but I found that the truth sets us free (John 8:32).

That popular Bible verse caused me to remember when Martin L. King, Jr. said, "Free at last, free at least, thank God Almighty we're free at last!" Perhaps, he meant that blacks were on their way to being treated like equal citizens in a country they had helped to build but weren't able to fully experience. They had been unable to partake of the benefits of a good education and the American dream due to discrimination. The Civil Rights movement had truly made the black community free at last because they could now enjoy privileges unprecedented in our country's history.

The freedom I desired went deeper, however, because I wanted to be free from all prejudices and past hates. I wanted to be able to speak my hurt as a black person and then get a response to begin my healing. With Sue I could do this. I was glad for Operation Oreo because it felt good to have someone to just listen, and she did.

Sue and I had always tried to demonstrate to our students that what we had together went beyond the surface in our friendship. The way we shared, interacted, and taught the interdisciplinary lessons we did on the Civil Rights era proved this. We once even applied for a grant for a program we entitled, "You Can't Judge a Book By Its Cover," seeking to expand our lesson and reach even more young people. However, when it was denied, we concluded that if not on a wide scale, we would continue to teach it in our classrooms and affect the future on a smaller scale. This message of learning to love, appreciate, or just recognize the differences among people would help those we taught to understand that we are still more alike than different. We all truly need to feel love and give love; feel appreciated and accepted to fulfill our purpose in this life.

I liked Sue's "Operation Oreo." Now what we had been doing all along had a cool name. She had experimented with what I call "selective segregation," where we choose to be with those who are most like us simply because we feel more comfortable or familiar with those people. I totally agree with Sue—all people are more alike than different, but we do have different cultures. People with similar cultures have a unique bond, and because there are those differences, we should seek to learn about and appreciate them. I believe the differences give us more spice in life.

It is just like the Bible said, "There is nothing new under the sun" (Ecclesiastes 1:9). In the 1960's another teacher, Jane Elliott, used differences in eye color to teach the concept of unwarranted discrimination to a group of elementary students through an experiment called the "Blue Eye/Brown Eye Exercise." A decade later in the 1970's, Coach Boone and Coach Yoast endured a similar situation in the Gettysburg College experience made popular in Disney's "Remember the Titans," starring Denzel Washington and Will Patton. Even before the movie's release, and twenty years later, Sue, in the early 1990's was inspired by God to bring about racial unity as had numerous unknown and unsung reformers before her. Each of these teachers was fighting the same battle: the age-old, demonic spirit of racism. But maybe now society would be ready for a major healing among the races. Since everything comes line upon line and precept upon precept, maybe now society could handle change within the races on a larger scale. Maybe Operation Oreo would catch on like the "Blue Eye/Brown Eye Exercise" concept to demonstrate that discrimination is very hurtful and wrong. Maybe, just maybe, Operation Oreo could be offered in other schools' extra-curricular or after school programs. Maybe Operation Oreo could be taken across the city, state, or nation by way of our classrooms, colleges, churches, and workplaces. Maybe, perhaps maybe, Operation Oreo could be the main platform upon which people of every race could begin to talk, learn about differences, agree to disagree, work out hard feelings, and grow as human beings. Perhaps, maybe . . . ?

"No one is born hating another person because of the
colour of his skin, or his background, or his religion. People
learn to hate, and if they can learn to hate, they can be taught
to love, for love comes more naturally to the human heart than
its opposite."
—Nelson Mandela

TWO VOICES AS ONE…FOR YOU

So many black people don't know how white people think, and white people don't understand the exuberance and feelings of blacks. Hispanics, Latinos, Asian groups, and others need to be included in this Operation Oreo mix because we have discovered that "black and white" is only the beginning. Other racial groups have faced similar discrimination and should be included if the healing process is to be effective. Understanding only comes from spending time with someone who is different from you. Until you get to know someone for real—get inside their "skin"—you will never bridge the gap between the races because you won't really know who the person is. Take a leap of faith and try it; you could be incredibly blessed as a result.

TEN YEARS LATER

Deidre's Voice:

After rereading what Sue and I had both written so long ago, I concluded how this chapter could easily combine the themes of "Operation Oreo" and "Must We Repeat History." More notably, as I began to look back over what I had said ten years ago, I began to feel so vulnerable. I couldn't believe how incredibly honest I had been about the O. J. verdict. Even though those brutal murders took place over twenty years ago in June of 1994, I now cringe at the mention of O. J. Simpson's name. I still believe, probably like most Americans, that O. J. did commit those notorious murders. He further sabotaged his badly damaged image and reputation as pre-publication controversy over his book entitled *If I Did It* went viral. The book reportedly recorded a hypothetically detailed account of how O. J. would have carried out the murders (**IF** he actually did it). I could no longer feel any justification for O. J. Simpson for any reason. Many Americans criticized him severely for a book that alarmingly suggested in a subtle, conniving way, "**SO WHAT** if I Did It."

Just as the original trial was full of chaos and showcased a three-ring circus that included the infamous Bronco chase and the household chant of "If it doesn't fit, you must acquit," even more confusion ensued once a former manager of O. J. Simpson by the name of Norman Pardo surfaced. He came forward explaining how O. J. was offered and ignorantly accepted $600,000 just to take credit for the book that was actually written by an anonymous author. This ghost writer supposedly used public records and several theories offered by the prosecutors to actually complete the book. The three-ring circus grew to a five-ring circus when Mr. Pardo went on public record stating that he had a legitimate copy of a letter from an inmate named Glen Rogers, a known serial killer, currently awaiting execution on death row in a Florida prison. He claimed that Roger's letter offered an apology to O. J. for taking his bad rap and included a confession for the murders of Nicole Brown Simpson and Ron Goldman. He said the letter was being held by the California DA and was available for public access and proof. The New York Post also aired a documentary on Glen Edward Rogers in 1996 with similar claims. Regardless of who actually committed this horrible crime, my heart still grieves for the Goldman family and for the two adult Simpson children.

Now 2014 echoes with this same domestic violence from the past as several other athletes and TV "stars" are being spotlighted and charged for domestic and spousal abuse. Perhaps, had more detail and prompt attention been given to these dire problems back when Nicole Brown Simpson first reported being viciously attacked, her death and some of these recent cases might have been avoided. How and when will this cycle of abuse end? Are we turning a deaf ear to the cries of the hurting? Do our eyes remain closed to the obvious appearance of pain and suffering?

Even as I update this chapter, that feeling of vulnerability is still a reality for me in regards to the O. J. case. It is twenty years later, and I have been made aware of more information surrounding the deaths of two beautiful and innocent people deeply missed by their families. Any attempt at being fair would require that I take all reports into consideration, but that is a difficult task once a mind is already made up on any given issue. Once again I asked myself, "Who would want to take an innocent mother away from her precious babies? Yes, a jealous husband could kill his wife out of anger but so could a serial killer ruthlessly slay an innocent man and famous mother due to his severed conscience. What if Glen Rogers is telling the truth about the fact that he did it? What if O. J. is really innocent? What if the media downplayed facts about the real murder and accentuated circumstances that made O. J. the easy target? What if a silent racial and social-economic plague still divides and conquers us with, "someone" has to pay?

Those unanswered questions caused me to reflect just a little more as I deliberated over the recent case involving the shooting of Michael Brown. I observed something similar to what Sue noticed ten years ago in the O. J. Simpson case, and that is that many white Americans appear to be looking at the case from a totally different perspective as do African-Americans. Even news stations have reported statements from the two sides differently. Three bystanders who claimed to have seen Michael Brown put his hands up stating, "Don't shoot," were shown, but most commentators continued to caution viewers that these alleged eye-witness reports were not yet proven as fact. However, when one lady commented on how she was not an eye-witness but represented the policeman who shot Brown, those same commentators displayed her comments as worthy to be treated as fact and continued to play her statement repeatedly. They also continued to run a video of Michael Brown bullying a shop owner to demonstrate his behavior. Yes, what that young man was doing was totally wrong, but you cannot display one act out of a person's day as if that is the total character of an individual. If any one of us had a camera recording us during a time when we were "not on our best behavior," we would not want that one time displayed as if it were the measure of our true or full character because "all have sinned." Still, many who oppose my opinion would state it demonstrates how Brown may have had a tendency to show belligerence to authority. This is also a valid point, but what about the actions of the policeman. For him to continue to shoot so many times seems unreasonable, just like the Jacksonville, FL case of Jordan Davis, who was shot multiple times as well. After that one shooting in Ferguson, we learned there were at least six more reported within a two-month-period where a cop or cops used excessive force against an unarmed black man. Some things are destined to remain inexplicable for whatever the reason. As long as we have incidents like or similar to this, the idea of Operation Oreo may be more difficult to spread than I originally thought ten years ago.

Perhaps the school setting is still the best place to reach a majority while their minds and brains are still developing, but the word of God has to remain the basis for any real improvement between the races. Racism does still exist in America, and I know it involves so many other races besides blacks and whites. After living in Japan for three years, I learned how the Japanese have had problems with the Koreans, both North and South. While relations have improved with Japan and South Korea, North Korea still will not acknowledge Japan as a country. Once I was getting my nails manicured and shared with the Vietnamese nail tech about my visit to Japan. I noticed her lack of enthusiasm over the Japanese culture when I began to respond so animatedly to her question, "How did you like it over there?" I finally asked her about the history of the two countries. Her reply was, "Not good." Admittedly ignorant regarding most Asian history, I did learn some important aspects about the Asian culture. I understood that she would say very little openly regarding her country's persecution because experience has taught me that Asians tend to be extremely reserved, calm, and discreet. Their respect for country, themselves, and others seems to be a priority for how they live. Later research revealed how the Vietnamese had suffered much persecution from the Japanese government, and that racism between the two cultures still exists.

I also saw recently on TV how many Japanese-Americans are finally becoming vocal about the mistreatment from their own government in the United States during WWII when many other non-Asian Americans feared that Japanese-Americans would turn against them after the attack on Pearl Harbor. Those anti-Asian attitudes led to internment camps, and they remind me of an incident in the chapter of Exodus in the Bible. The pharaoh of Joseph's time readily welcomed the house of Israel (Jacob) and his descendants to leave Canaan, come live in Egypt and prosper during a time of famine. Years later, a different pharaoh came on the throne who knew nothing about Joseph's people, culture, or his relationship with the former Egyptian king. He began to fear the numerous growth and wealth of its foreign inhabitants (the Israelites), so he persecuted them with harsh labor and even death. History does repeat again and again, and we are reminded that fear is apparently the problem every ethnicity has experienced. Fear remains a major factor in promoting racial problems with different cultures.

This only further proves what I stated earlier about how we need more wide-spread and open forums for all races of people to discuss our differences and help us with our areas of ignorance. For example, I had to correct many of my students for believing it was all right to refer to every Asian person as Chinese; they didn't know any better. We must impact the lives of many in a huge way and further continue the process of healing. This healing can only come from the one true "Balm in Gilead" (the healing power of Jesus), and it will help move us more expediently towards understanding the basic premise of Operation Oreo that states, "We are more alike than different." The Bible proves it in Genesis 1:27 (KJV): "So God created man in His own image, in the image of God created He him, male and female created He them."

Operation Oreo—here we come! Please join us.

Sue's Voice:

This is one of my favorite chapters because it brings back fond memories. In rereading Deidre's **Voice I** account, it struck me that these events happened in the early 1990s. I am now writing in 2014—how is that possible! Time has, indeed, marched on, but over twenty years later, I can still see the reactions that inspired me to experiment with Operation Oreo. I remember walking through that crowded cafeteria and joining in with students who were having fun and learning a lesson at the same time—the textbook definition of a "teachable moment" that will remain with me forever. Did my students learn anything of lasting value? Or has life and family experiences reinforced racial stereotypes that continue to divide instead of unite? I will never know, but I did the best I could to introduce them to a concept that I hope they continued in their lives—that of acceptance and inclusion.

Unfortunately, we are reminded of division with many situations in everyday life. How many of you remember taking standardized tests in school and filling out the personal information prior to taking the actual test: name, age, birth date, and racial background? Have any teachers reading this chapter ever had a student puzzled as to what to bubble in on that last category? I think the info page might contain an "other" category now which could serve those students who are racially mixed or consider themselves different from those listed. My point is—why is this category necessary? I know, for record-keeping and comparisons. I still find it annoying!

All right, let me move to another example. When you fill out a credit application or apply for a bank loan, why is your ethnicity necessary on the form? Isn't your credit score and income history sufficient and really more important? As much as we try to move forward and make race something that is not an important qualifier in life, it smacks us right in the forehead time and time again. So has anything really changed over the passage of time since I attempted to show eighth graders that race is not that important? Frustrating, isn't it!

I also remember when our first version of **Small Voices** was published, Deidre and I were scheduling book signings throughout the Hampton Roads area of Virginia. My Sunday School class seemed very interested when I shared about the book, even praying for and helping supply a publisher for us. However, when "push came to shove," the invitation for a Sunday School book signing we had previously discussed was mysteriously removed after the wife of our teacher read an advanced copy. I accepted her change of heart without question, but always wondered if this lady from the South was uncomfortable with some of the inclusionary content.

Many people, including some in my own family deny that racism still exists today with all the sweeping legal changes. I recently read a *Time* magazine article by basketball legend Kareem Abdul-Jabbar which quoted both him and Donald Sterling, the Los Angeles Clippers owner who lost his team when his taped racist statements became public knowledge. In this article, entitled "How to Tell if You Are a Racist," Abdul-Jabbar said, "Racism today isn't like the racism pre-Martin Luther King, Jr. Today we are faced with 'situational racism'—that is, people must act according to a realistic analysis of race as it is in our society right now, not as they wish it were . . . that's what Donald Sterling meant when he said on tape, 'It's the world!' We don't evaluate what's right and wrong, we live in a society . . . a culture. I don't want to change the culture because I can't. It's too big!' He didn't see his attitude as racist—just a practical reaction to a racist world." Additionally Abdul-Jabbar stated, "Maybe the worst racism of all is denying that racism exists."

All you have to do is look around you to realize that Operation Oreo is still needed today. News items show us how divided we still are when it comes to matters of race as both Deidre and I have mentioned in previous chapters. Even though mixed-race couples in society, shown in prom pictures, or holding hands on college campuses are not as unusual or shocking as they appeared in earlier generations, understanding or acceptance is far from the norm. Would that be the case if more people would get to know and better understand those who look different from them? It's the same question I asked those eighth graders so many years ago, who were willing to accept the challenge to get to know classmates in a better way. They were pleased with the results and so was I.

Deidre has raised some serious questions in her TYL section. How many of us live our lives in distrust or fear of people who are different than we are? Are our police departments and courts flawed in respect to how they treat minorities versus whites? Many think so and if that is true, does this situation stem from never learning about other races in a way that breaks down barriers. We are who we are, but we can change our perceptions through education. This education comes from experience with others. There are many white people that I want to avoid, so why wouldn't I realize that there will be black, brown, and other races of people that "do not float my boat?" That doesn't make me a racist; just someone who prefers to select friends and acquaintances based on shared likes and dislikes. There's no reason why someone of a different race wouldn't share those qualities. This entire chapter is meant to encourage others to consider our similarities rather than our differences.

We will always live with those who want to remain in their own comfort zone among people in social or business sectors. I understand that. Sadness is the first emotion that comes to my mind when I consider these people. They are missing out on a lot by refusing to cross the line into unfamiliar territory. We will never come together and love as God wants us to until we realize that our "neighbor" may be someone that crosses income, racial, and neighborhood boundaries. It's never easy to make that first tentative start into a new situation, but you might be surprised at what you learn and how much you enjoy it.

CHAPTER X

"Acting White" — An Inside Story of Academic Underachievement

"Today parents and educators must combat the perverse view among many black kids that serious scholarship is a <u>white thing</u>."
—*John Ogbu, University of California* *

Voice II:

I was always a good student. I tried hard and worked to fix what I perceived was lacking in my academic life. When I attended college to become a teacher, I had no idea that many of my future students wouldn't approach their studies in a like manner. Regardless of race or gender, many students today seem to lack the inner work ethic or willingness to do well in school. This is why educators, administrators, and school systems are continually coming up with external motivators like pizza parties, gift certificates, and honor roll celebrations to encourage students to work harder and perform better. This lack of student motivation really surprised me when I entered the classroom as a new teacher. I felt that if I did my job to present the material in an interesting and stimulating way, the students would be encouraged and want to learn.

Over the years my idealism has faded somewhat, and I have learned that this doesn't always happen with many students whose main interests are their sports activities and social life. For them school is only a place to see and be seen. In their book, *No Excuses: Closing the Racial Gap in Learning*, Abigail and Stephen Thernstrom ** point out that nearly 25% of all students leave high school with academic skills that are "Below Basic." This means that the NAEP (National Assessment of Educational Progress) rates them as unable to show even a partial mastery of knowledge and skills that are necessary for passing work at their grade level. If you look at one individual category, African-American students, the picture gets even worse. Forty percent of the black students score below basic in writing, 70% do so in math, science results are 75% lower than basic, with history and geography test scores no better. This means that employers of many black high school graduates are actually hiring people who perform just a little better than eighth graders in both reading and U. S. history, and even worse in math and geography. Regardless of the category, the unending challenge remains: how do you awaken the clueless clients, our students, to the necessity of using their time wisely to prepare themselves for high school and their futures?

Every year throughout my years of teaching, I have continually sought to encourage students to do their best, not only in sports, the arts, or other interests, but also in the classroom. I try to show them through stimulating quotes, newspaper articles, and the examples of others, that hard work in school really pays off later when they are accepted into college, a university, the military, or training programs that will allow them to live a good life and be of help to others. However, I never expected to encounter a baffling, infuriating mindset held by some African-American students which they called "acting white."

I first discovered this situation while teaching eighth graders several years after I began my teaching career. A very attractive black student came to me in tears over comments that had been made to her in the hall of our school. She said that some of the other popular black girls in her group had told her that if she made the Honor Roll again, they would drop her from their group because they had no respect for their people who "acted white." When I asked her what they meant, she shook her head and told me, "I'm still trying to figure it out." Never one to stop when there's a question to be answered, I plunged into this confusing situation and was dumbfounded by the responses I heard. It seemed that succeeding in school was seen by a number of black students as a "white" thing to do. They saw the black role in school to be sports, music, dancing, and the social scene. Where they excelled naturally and easily, they ruled. However, in the classroom, where good grades required a lot more work and effort, it was easier to dismiss this challenging area as the domain of white students. While "white men can't jump," they could learn math formulas, and where white girls "had no rhythm," they could test better than the black dance queens. I tried to counter this type of thinking with the idea that there was once a time when Michael Jordan had never touched a basketball and had no idea how to dunk. It took a lot of work, practice, and will-power for #23 to achieve all that he did to become the top at his game, and Michael actually graduated with a BA degree from the University of North Carolina in 1986. Why couldn't my students decide to go for academics with the same work ethic?

Not all of my students grasped this type of thinking. However, a majority did understand the idea that many things do not come easily at first, but with hard work, determination, and the unwillingness to give up, improvement will definitely come. They could note the comparison or similarity with sports. Many of my students remembered when they began to play football, basketball, hockey, soccer, or began cheering. The moves, plays, and confidence weren't there in the beginning, but steadily improved with practice and experience. Nothing pleases me more as a teacher than to see a student slowly but surely improve in my class. Moving from a "D" the first nine weeks to a "B" by the end of the year is a dramatic change and a true lesson in life. Hard work does pay off regardless of the area of involvement.

Whether my underachievers are black, white, Hispanic, Asian, or mixed-race and characterized as gifted, advanced, average, or low ability, this is a lesson that is so important to learn. I hope I have taught it as well as I have taught history. The old cliché is correct: "If at first you don't succeed, try, try again." I have added to it a quote from Verne Hill which says: "If you always do what you've always done, you'll always get what you always got." This aptly states that you have to change your method if you aren't satisfied with the results. Additionally, you have to understand that you are a person, an individual with gifts that require work to shine. Don't ever allow yourself to be characterized as a race or a group (see Ch. VII). You are responsible to yourself, your family, and to God—not your friends. One day they will go their way and you will go yours. Why would you allow them to define you today? Don't act black or white, grunge or hip-hop, just be "yourself" and try your best to develop what God gave you at birth. Your fingerprints are unique and so are you, so work hard to develop your special talents!

* Black American Students in an Affluent Suburb: A Study of Academic Disengagement
** Cited by Walter E. Williams, John M. Olin Professor of Economics at George Mason University in his editorial, "No Excuses for Students Failing in School"

Voice I:

I agree wholeheartedly with Sue. I have overheard students yell out phrases like: "She's acting white," when an African-American student chooses to use standard English and ignore commonly used slang, such as "We be tired," or "She wear them clothes too much," and "He wants to be black" because a white classmate listens to rap music and wears the hip-hop clothing associated with black culture. Several years ago, Sue shared with me the term "whigger" which meant "a white person who acts black." These students seemed to admire the music, clothing, and style of the black culture and easily adopted it as their own. Is it surprising then that some black students are seen by their peers as trying to act white when they choose and enjoy making good grades and give this a priority?

I believe that some black students associate making good grades more with the white culture because in their homes education wasn't held in high esteem as the parents were so busy just trying to make ends meet and provide for their families. Traditionally within the black culture, more homes were parented by single working moms who struggled to pay bills and put food on the table with little time for reading stories and teaching about colors and shapes to their pre-school children. Statistics show that this problem still occurs today because the majority of children needing Head Start services through-out our country continue to be among the minority races. Many of these parents consistently put more emphasis on sports, shoes, name brand clothing, and music over books and education because, I believe, they view these things as the ticket out of poverty and into the good life. Why else is it that I have seen so many black students come to school with expensive name brand clothing and shoes, but without their homework or even their textbooks. Moreover, parents scramble to put their children in recreational sports programs at younger and younger ages, but show little to no support for school programs, such as PTA meetings, back-to-school nights, or teacher conferences. It will be difficult to change these mindsets as long as people can see sports figures and musical stars making millions of dollars more than doctors, lawyers, accountants, and engineers. As I have mentioned before, many little black boys dream of the NFL and NBA (see Ch. VIII) and see themselves as future stars there. As a matter of fact, years ago Sue taught one eighth grader who made his dream come true in the NBA.

When I first came to Davis Middle School, I remember Sue talking about this student she had taught the previous year who was so talented athletically and artistically. She was concerned because he had so many challenges in his life, and wasn't doing well academically. The promise was there, but would it be fulfilled? She continued to attend his games, write him notes of encouragement, send him McDonald's coupons, and even drop by his high school to see him before important play-off games. She wanted me to speak to him because we shared the one thing that they didn't—our race. When I met him one day, I told Sue that he was a good-looking kid as she had told me, but I felt that he was too cocky to listen to me at the time. Perhaps, years later the day would come when he would realize and appreciate what she was trying to do for him. Today, #3 on the 76ers has made his millions in the arena of basketball, but I wonder if Allen Iverson realizes that his eighth grade social studies teacher still thinks about him, prays for him, and wishes him success in life, not just on the basketball court.

He made it, but very few little boys do. That is why it is so important that they learn that education—not sports—is the key to their futures. Education provides more opportunities which in turn will allow individuals to enjoy a better lifestyle or provide the means for supporting themselves and their family. I would advise that you take advantage of public education through high school, and look for opportunities to fund your way through higher education by scholarships, grants, and loans. While it's good to have other dreams and goals, they aren't always fulfilled. However, education is something that can never be taken away from you.

"It's a Black thing, you wouldn't understand" is just as much an obsolete phrase as "She's acting white" and "He's acting black" should be. If a person chooses to enjoy the culture of another race, that is simply their choice and should not be met with condemnation and ridicule by others. As a race, the human race, we are all connected. After all, it really is just "a love thing."

TWO VOICES AS ONE...FOR YOU

Over the years there have been times when we have seen students doing much less than we know they could do. They allow peers to negatively influence their education without realizing the lifelong impact it will have. They are willing to get up early and wait in line at the mall for the latest sports star's tennis shoe, but they rarely have the same motivation for their academic life. Somehow we have to make both students and parents understand that the same energy and involvement young people invest in sports, music, and shopping for clothes has to find its way into the classroom as well.

The United Negro College Fund's motto is "A mind is a terrible thing to waste." We agree—why would you even consider it?

TEN YEARS LATER

Deidre's Voice:

In 2014, I believe, the true pressure to stop "acting black" or "acting white" has absorbed itself into a new struggle—the need for a lot of young people to act, look, dress, and become like their favorite actor, actress, singer, dancer, or athlete. This seems to be their top priority because they want to act and look like the athletes they see on TV and the performers who sing and dance in the music videos. Whatever you see the popular athletes and stars wearing and doing, that is who so many of our young people are now "acting like." When young people desire to display so many tattoos and piercing on their bodies until they look like walking murals or pieces of art work, they do not realize how ridiculous they look to the average individual living a normal lifestyle. The majority of athletes and TV stars live and move in totally different circles from most people. Many youth do not realize they are not a part of those inner circles. The stars they desire to emulate will only enjoy that luxury of freedom of expression for a season.

I remember that Sue shared with me how Allen Iverson had told her he looked forward to taking on Michael Jordan once he made it to the big leagues. He was in her eighth grade class during that time, and that big dream did become a reality. Yet that fame and fortune allowed him only a temporary pass into that "circle" that left almost as quickly as it had come. Allen and many other basketball athletes were a part of that bold move towards open and large displays of tattooing. Many football players also helped usher in and promote this latest fad of tattooing an entire arm, leg, and half of their body. That style of body art is so current that no one really knows the horrors that might eventually surface when those same individuals grow old—if they get to grow older. We just do not know.

These "acting-like-famous people" youngsters believe they can get instant fame and fortune through hits on YouTube, Twitter, and InstaGram. They further fantasize about quick fame and fortune by dreaming of participating in talent search shows made popular today through venues like "America's Got Talent," "The Voice," "American Idol," "Sunday's Best," and "So You Think You Can Dance." Additionally, most TV and music videos continually display how sexuality is now an individual's preference. Our students and young adults are shown or told they have a choice to be heterosexual, bisexual, homosexual, a-sexual, or super-freaky sexual, depending on their own individual preference. Many decent examples of what is moral, proper and correct have disappeared completely as many Americans have taken God's standard out of everything.

Education is still widely promoted as the key ingredient to a healthy, happy, and successful lifestyle, but for many young people, school is still a place for socialization and a display of fashion trends along with a lack of respect for adults and other authority figures. There also remain more African-Americans and Hispanics who continue to perform lower than their White and Asian counterparts on standardized testing. There are many studies and statistics available on the high school drop-out rate, illiteracy, teenage pregnancy, AIDS, incarceration, low standardized test scores, and low school performance for any state, city, or other type of demographics. Sadly, as an African-American, it still bothers me that a huge portion of these reports place blacks as the majority in most, if not all of these categories. Some are only true for certain demographics and others will continue to remain that way due to cultural differences and a perpetual cycle that began with the history of our country. However, all of our country's history and its social problems need to be dealt with brutally, openly, and honestly through dialogue. The ills this country suffers are not few in number. It remains full of pedophiles; husbands who kill their wives for insurance money or simply because they want a different spouse; children who kill parents or grandparents when they don't accept a boyfriend, girlfriend or lifestyle; human-traffic offenders; cops who kill unarmed men; drug lords who bring huge quantities of heroin, cocaine, and marijuana into our country's borders to distribute and sell; doctors convicted of Medicare and insurance fraud; students who will cheat on a college entry test to get accepted into an Ivy League school; federal building bombings; school and public shoot-outs; and attacks on the White House. The list is endless here in America, but who or what determines what facts, data, or social problems get reported more than others?

The crux of the matter remains that Americans are viewed as one people and one country by many foreigners who vehemently hate us with open-contempt. We will rise and fall as a nation; so any part of America that is weak or "broken" impacts us all. It's time to demand an open-forum on "acting and being an American." Perhaps open and honest dialogue can begin with the following:

What has happened to divide all of the different races of people who live in our country and consider themselves Americans?

What are some root causes for the many gaps and feelings of mistrust between different races?

What can we as individuals do to help heal our land?

Can we agree on a definition of what it means to be an American for all of the different races and cultures of people living here?

What does "take back America" really mean?

Every American needs to feel good about and proud to be a part of this country so he or she can really feel like one and not have to pretend to "act American." Christians need to unite on a larger scale and take our country back for the glory of God because that is the basis of who we really are: "ONE NATION UNDER GOD!"

Sue's Voice:

Only in a middle school/high school mind could an Honor Roll celebration be a cause for exclusion from the group! I couldn't believe what I was hearing those years ago when my sweet eighth grade student was tearfully trying to understand why she had to choose between academic achievement and peer acceptance. Since I have been retired from the classroom for almost ten years, I can't say whether this school situation still exists as we have described it, but I wouldn't be surprised if it does. In fact, I read an article posted on Facebook (Addicting Info Website) recently which gave me an insightful perspective from retired NBA player and sports commentator, Charles Barkley. In an interview with Philadelphia radio station 94 WIP, Barkley ranted against the black community's "dirty, dark secret" and opened up to expose it. He is quoted as saying the following, "As I tell my white friends, we as black people, we're never going to be successful, not because of you white people, but because of other black people. When you're black, you have to deal with so much crap in your life from other black people. It's a dirty, dark secret; I'm glad it's coming out. . . . I said, you know, when young black kids, you know, when they do well in school, the loser kids tell them, 'Oh, you're acting white.' The kids who speak intelligently . . . they tell them, 'You're acting white.' So it's a dirty, dark secret in the black community. . . . . And for some reason we are brainwashed to think, if you're not a thug or an idiot, you're not black enough. . . . I heard Stephen A. (Smith) talking about it, and, listen, I hate to bring white people into our crap, but as a black person, we all go through it when you're successful." Well, there you go! I couldn't explain it any better.

Peer influence is a mighty motivator for good or bad among many people. When you think about it, some adults still perform to the beat of their peers' drums. Clothing purchases, club dates, movie and music choices, preferred neighborhood home buys all point to the fact that many of us still look to others for life's leads. What does that say about the confidence we have within ourselves to make choices that are the best for us and our families?

Character and maturity come with experience and age . . . or do they? You would think that adults would have grown up enough to not follow where others lead. However, if we feel we need additional help in making life's choices, where should we look for help in making them?

Family is always a good place to start. This is where you began and you can expect to find good advice because most parents look out for their children. Wait a minute! Maybe years ago that would have been a good idea, but take a look at some of our families today and you might change your mind. Multiple marriages, substance abuse charges, parents not parenting—you get the idea. Not all families would be a good place to go.

Maybe lifelong friends could lead us in the right path. It all depends—how are those friends doing with their lives? Is the "party girl" still living for Friday night and the club? Does the jock still gravitate towards the stadium or the sports bar, beer bottle in hand? Is your former college roommate still trying to get his/her life and credit together? None of these things are bad in and of themselves as an infrequent event, but if this is the lifestyle of your friends, I advise you to skip their example.

I was fortunate to have been raised in the 50's/60's within a strict household with a mother and father who had high expectations, tolerated little disobedience, and took me to church weekly. I learned at an early age that following the Golden Rule and the Ten Commandments was the right thing to do and would benefit me greatly in life. Guess what? It's still working! I try my best to treat others as I wish to be treated, avoid lying, haven't killed anyone yet, and don't take God's name in vain. These lifelong habits didn't help me become a member of the popular group in high school, but you know what, that group is highly overrated. It's amazing what you learn when you return for a 25-yr. or later reunion. Cheerleaders have put on weight, some class officers are still trying to find that "job," and the most successful classmates seem to be among the ones who worked hard in school, and were largely ignored by the "beautiful people." I'm not trying to be bitter or judgmental here, I'm just trying to convey what I observed. I'm very glad I wasn't accepted into that popular group. I might not have had the ability to resist all the temptations that would have come with those associations. God had a plan for me and it has worked out for the good.

I would like to suggest that anyone reading my words check out Jeremiah 29:11 in the Old Testament. It reads, "For I know the plans I have for you, declares the Lord, plans to prosper you and not to harm you, plans to give you hope and a future." God has, indeed, been faithful, and has led my husband and me through good times as well as difficult ones. Hindsight is always 20/20, but as I look back, I wouldn't change much of what I have experienced. I have tried to remain true to my teachings and lived my life being ME. That's my advice to you. As we said in Ch. IV, be YOU. Don't let anyone else lead you in the wrong way. The words I spoke to that confused eighth grader years ago, still ring true today, "Don't let anyone else make decisions for you. Decide to do what makes you and your family proud and moves you forward in life." I dare say that the Honor Roll list is a far better achievement than friendship with those who can't or won't make it. Even Charles Barkley called those people "losers." In the end, it's all up to you. What do you think?

> "Some succeed because they are destined to, but most succeed
> because they are determined to."
> —Henry van Dyke

CHAPTER XI

Shame on You

"There is a way that seems right to a man, but in the end,
it leads to death."
—Proverbs 14:12

Voice II:

I am writing this chapter after viewing news clips yesterday of the latest MTV award show which among other things broadcast an "open mouth" kiss between three women. This is just the latest example of the wasteland of television programming that is available to the American public, both young and old. On prime time programming today you can view sexual situations, hear profanity and God's name taken in vain repeatedly, see young people totally disrespect their parents in family sitcoms, watch shocking, disgusting events on reality shows, and ogle gyrating, partially-clad females in music videos while the male singer/rapper uses derogatory names for them right in their presence. *

Some cultural experts say this is one reason why our country is reviled in fundamentalist countries in the Middle East and other places around the world. They view our movies and television programs, and judge all Americans by what they see. Did the decadence on the small and large screens lead to 9-11? You be the judge. The more troubling observation might be that regardless of which countries see us as the Great Satan or an infidel nation due to perceived immorality, our children are growing up accepting what they see and hear on television and movies as appropriate behavior that they want to copy.

Over the last thirty to forty years, movies have become much more violent and sexually explicit. In order to receive an "R" rating which means a bigger cross-over audience and more profits, movie producers make sure there are several bedroom scenes or profanity-laden dialogue or over-the-top graphic violence. Some movies showcase all of these in a visual smorgasbord of smut. Like the proverbial frog (see Ch. VI, TYL, Sue), we have been slowly but surely "cooked to death" by the ever-increasing level of things we formerly wouldn't have accepted, but now have seen so much of that we don't even think to protest. However, television and movies are only the beginning of the negative influences affecting our children.

Have you tried to buy attractive but suitable and age-appropriate clothing for girls lately? I don't know who is designing outfits for young ladies in this new millennium, but I think they are stuck with the "Lolita look," even in elementary school. Bared midriffs, low-riding jeans, thongs, tee-strapped tops, stretchy body-clinging outfits, and shorts so short that they are probably a health hazard! It doesn't take much detective work to deduce that these types of clothing that hang in most department and discount stores are based on designs worn by the pop music divas. When the eight to thirteen-year-old Britney, Christina, and Kim "wannabes" walk the halls of their schools, they end up looking totally out of place and downright promiscuous. Maybe that's why some of our male students have trouble concentrating in school! I have to question why more parents don't refuse to buy these clothes. The excuse that "everybody's wearing it," or "I won't fit in" just doesn't work for me. These are your daughters— why would you send them out in public looking like street walkers?

If pop music styles affect the way the girls dress, you only have to look on the other side of the hall to see a similar problem with the male wardrobe. The hip hop craze caught on years ago, with baggy pants, multi-layered clothing, gang-suggesting bandanas, "bling" jewelry, and a "rolling" stroll complete with constantly gyrating arms. School has become a place to show-case how well you can copy the latest fad from the world of music videos, not a place to do well academically.

Speaking of music, young people have always loved music, and so do I. But if I turn on the cable music channels, the images ruin my appreciation for the tune or rhythm. Then when I decipher the lyrics on some songs, I just get angry. There seem to be no boundaries as to what is said or sung. I teach social studies, so I am familiar with the freedom of speech argument. The Ku Klux Klan used it for years as they spewed their garbage to the public. When people stopped listening, their influence started to die. In the case of the musical refuse, I just keep thinking that my students, my children, Godchildren, and other young people might be listening to these words, and if so, their minds are being filled with images that are not good for them. People might ask who am I to judge the creativity of another? I would answer that I am an adult who recognizes obscenity when it occurs, either in images or words.

The computer, one of the most life-changing inventions for America and the world during the last generation, has become an area of danger for our young people, and, indeed, everyone. Pornography is readily available in our living rooms, family rooms, or even our teenagers' bedrooms because there are estimated to be seven million X-rated Websites available online. Advertisements for these sites pop up on everyone's e-mail addresses giving anyone who is interested, any kind of filth or perversion they might desire. Not just beastiality or bondage, but child porn. These types of shocking pictures rob our children of what little innocence they might possess at younger and younger ages. We are living in an age of spiritual darkness and desperately need more people to step up and shed some light for those who are lost by fighting against these types of websites.

This leads me back to the title of this chapter. Shame on you pop, rap, hip hop, and other musical stars who are leading America's young people astray and pocketing millions of dollars by doing so! I know—my generation had Elvis and the Beatles who were shocking in their day—but did you ever see them star in the type of music videos shown on MTV and BET any hour of the day? The very fact that the recent awards show had to resort to a demonstration of lesbian kisses during a musical number for shock value shows just how far down the ladder of moral decay we have come. Any thinking American knows that type of act would never have gotten out of the strip joints or peep shows a few years ago.

When does it stop? How far will it go? Why shouldn't a holy God be ready to destroy us as He did Sodom and Gomorrah for their increasing immorality? These are serious questions for serious times, but the underlying reason for my questions remains. How can any of these things I have mentioned have a positive effect on our children and young people? They are becoming hardened to all manner of things that are offensive to many of us, wanting even more violence, sexuality, profanity, carnality, and gore. Everyone who has contributed to this immoral entertainment industry will one day be held accountable.

As for now, it's time for adults who care to begin to speak out, petition our elected leaders, and stop allowing the liberal media, press, and organizations to continue to push the envelope on what we will legally allow in this country (see Ch. XII). Parents, get serious about doing your job as a mom or dad, and realize that sometimes you have to draw the line on what you will accept in your children's lives because their futures are at stake! Remember, regardless of their ages, your sons and daughters will always be your children. They will grow up and make choices based on what they saw, heard, and learned under your roof.

I hope they make you proud!

Voice I:

"Who let the dogs out?" "Back that thing up . ." "I like big butts . ." "It's getting hot in here, so take off all your clothes!"

These are not the familiar lyrics that I want to hear playing in my teenager's room. Yet, some in society see these as fun and entertaining tunes, even using them on TV and radio as messages to promote an interesting way of life. I am so ashamed at how many of these videos offered on TV show our youth how to dress in such provocative and disgusting clothing. Some even fall into the false perception that certain groups of people are sex-crazed and sex-driven freaks. These videos send the message that all these types of people can do is party, drive lavishly expensive cars, make babies, and play ball. Aside from being ashamed, I'm angry, and the objects of my anger are those in the black community who have allowed my race to be stereotyped in this way.

So I turn off the TV and go to the mall to enjoy a shopping experience with my daughter. It is a sad day when all I can find in popular department stores are low-cut tops and tight, hip-hugger pants to buy her for back to school. Many clothes I saw in the stores seemed to scream, "Here it is—come and get it!" Wake up people—put down your basketballs and pick up a good book! Bump and grind and shaking your "booty" should not be the theme of your life because you have far more talents than that. As you read and learn about history, you will discover that many African-Americans, as well as people from other ethnic groups, come from a fine legacy of doctors, lawyers, inventors, builders, and military heroes. You could join that list of outstanding Americans if only you cared about your future as much as you do about the latest songs, fashions, and dances.

If any group of people wants to change how they are viewed by society, they are the ones who must play a major role in that transformation. It is time for us to make things happen for ourselves. We must use the human resources that God places in our lives. Don't look at the package or the color in which it comes; just look for your lifelines because they are out there. All you need is to just find one, and I know you have them because God put them there. People of all color are told by God in His word that "we are the lenders and not the borrowers," "the head and not the tail," and "above and not beneath." (Deut. 28:12-13). Seek to serve your fellow man first, and your needs will be met naturally because it's God's law and it works.

I want to challenge everyone to work hard and bring society to what should be our best music in life. Instead of "dogs," "butts," and "heat," those popular lyrics that drag us down to our base levels, the most pressing concern should be those things that elevate us as a people not degrade us as a group. As long as we allow anything, our nation will continue to fall. Remember, Rome was destroyed from within by its immorality. Will America follow suit? As one familiar and wise cliché states, "You have to stand for something, or you will fall for anything!" In my opinion, our country is falling rapidly because too few people are willing to speak out against anything. Galatians 6:9-10 encourages us to stand strong saying:

"Let us not be weary in doing good; for at the proper time, we will reap a harvest if we do not give up. Therefore, as we have opportunity, let us do good."

This should be the tune and theme of our lives: united we must stand for righteousness or divided we <u>will</u> fall. The lyrics to one of my favorite Winan songs sums it up perfectly:

"I remember when life was so simple
You did or you didn't,
You would or you wouldn't
But it ain't like that anymore.
I remember when life was so easy
People said what they meant—they were either for it or
     against,
But it ain't like that anymore.
Somewhere we lost the score.
I remember when life was so simple
Boys grew into men,
Little girls to women then.
But it ain't like that anymore.
I remember when life was so easy
Parents were the light
Through them we saw what was right.
But it ain't like that anymore.
Somewhere we lost the score
Bring back the days of 'Yay and Nay'
When we could plainly see the way
When it was up to us to choose whether to win or lose.
Bring back the time when we could see
What it was we were to be,
Caught in the midst of complexity

We search for "Yay and Nay."
We knew where we belonged,
What was right and what was wrong
Bring back the days . . . . . ."

Bring Back the Days of "Yay and Nay"—The Winans

TWO VOICES AS ONE...FOR YOU

Shame is sometimes a good thing when it results in changed behavior. Even though the media, department stores, and the computer make so many negative things available today, parents and guardians still have the final choice in what they allow. It is our hope in this chapter to awaken readers to the fact that what parents allow in their home in the form of television, videos, clothing, and behavior is reflected in their children. Teenagers may resent hearing, but do understand the phrase, "Garbage in . . . garbage out." It's time for us as adults—the parents, teachers, leaders, and pastors—to dump the garbage in the can and leave it there so it doesn't affect the lives of the next generation. We have been told to "train up a child in the way he should go" (Proverbs 22:6), and not allow him to find his own way through trial and error or fall into the excuse that "everyone else is doing it."

Too many children are raising themselves . . . and too many parents are allowing it.

*[As this book goes to press (2004), the FCC is investigating Super Bowl XXXVIII's half-time show where up to 100 million people witnessed split second nudity during a musical number. FCC's chief Michael Powell is quoted as saying, "I am outraged at what I saw. Like millions of Americans, my family and I gathered around the televi-

sion for a celebration. Instead that celebration was tainted by a class-less, crass, and deplorable stunt. Our nation's children, parents, and citizens deserve better."]

"Preach the Word; be prepared in season and out of season; correct, rebuke, and encourage . . . For the time will come when men will not put up with sound doctrine. Instead, to suit their own desires, they will gather around them a great number of teachers to say what their itching ears want to hear. They will turn their ears away from the truth and turn aside to myths."—2 Timothy 4:24

TEN YEARS LATER

Deidre's Voice:

While we as Christians were sleeping, the enemy crept in stealthily and attacked us on every corner of our chambers. The shame fell on us as we hid behind the four walls of our individual church buildings. The places we so affectionately refer to as "my church" kept us oblivious to the presence of others including the entire household of faith known as Christendom. We snoozed on into a further state of slumber while God was telling us to unite as one body. We covered ourselves in blankets of comfort within our own denominations, ignoring churches plagued with racial divide and doctrinal differences. We focused more on church programs in order to raise money for additional modern upgrades on buildings already sufficient for kingdom building. We thought better lights, cameras, and stage appeal would draw in larger crowds and garner the attention of the millennial generation. As we continued to daydream about adding more people to our pews and a plethora of programs to our calendars, we forgot the most important message of all time. That message came from Jesus when he told us to just lift Him up before men, and people would come because He would draw them. We forgot to consistently love others as ourselves by feeding and clothing the needy, encouraging the hurting, and blessing the poor and the imprisoned. If only we would truly unite as one, then the commanded blessing would fall on the entire body of Christ and true provision for the ministry would be made available. The pattern for provision was already given to us in the book of Acts. Yet, we yawned and waved at it, and our eyes automatically closed to the truth because so many of us were weary from our individual works of faithfulness.

As individuals, we have knelt down beside our beds and forsook the proverbial, "Now I lay me down to sleep, I pray the Lord my soul to keep . . ." We stopped asking God to keep us and we began trying to keep ourselves. Still in our own state of sleep and slumber, we became warm and cozy with regular petitions to God for "me, my four, and no more." We continued to rest on our own accomplishments while boasting on the works we have performed for the sake of the ministry. We didn't want to share a bedroom with our siblings in Christ. We acted just like the world as we selfishly told God how we needed our own space because our needs are so different, and we don't want our little brothers and sisters of the faith messing with our "stuff." We proudly chose to close our own bedroom doors with silent signs of "DO NOT ENTER," or "FOR SAINTS ONLY," so outsiders would know to just, "KEEP OUT!" We demanded to have our own room! We made a conscious effort to remain behind the comforting four walls of our own church buildings still full of racial divide, partially due to our country's history and further separated by denominational differences. While we closed and locked the entry doors to our buildings, we did the same to the chambers of our hearts.

We treated our demands as if they were needs rather than wants. We lay or stood before a Holy God as if He, the ultimate Father, could not or would not provide for His own.

While we were sleeping, the "new normal" crept in and is now dominating every facet of our daily lives—our education, politics, family and sadly, even the church. Ten years ago, Sue mentioned the "open-mouth" kiss between three women on MTV. Today it is a regular occurrence on all basic TV, commercials, and cable shows. One such show, "Scandal," portrays marriage as a convenience for promotion rather than the sacred covenant God intended. The lead character is shown having hot and steamy sex scenes with the President of the United States, and the President's top aide is a man who has a husband. "The Good Wife" also widely displays adultery, homosexuality, bisexuality, and other "fun" conniving behavior on a regular basis. Another award-winning show, "Modern Family," has completely torn down the main fundamental ideas of a family, and the long-running "Family Guy" cartoon show is full of debauchery with few "family" values. Then, in between those types of shows, they show you commercials with a big potato eating a bag of potato chips or a square cinnamon piece of cereal eating other cereal of its same kind, and even a dog engaged in a full-open mouth attack on a man in an ad for chewing gum! I find none of these shows and advertisements cute or amazing. I believe at its base, these commercials are a form of perverted cannibalism and subliminally condition young viewers to embrace the idea of "eating" your own kind. I know that sounds far-fetched, but I totally understand how satan is going for the jugulars of the saints, while we who should know better, allow it.

We are experiencing the effect of a Pandora's box in our culture. For example, once the movie, "Brokeback Mountain" was released in 2005, I believe, a spirit of sympathy for the perverted was also released.

TV, movies, and music now encourage its viewers to sympathize with those practicing acts of homosexuality, adultery, hatred, witchcraft, and perversion. I know God was not pleased with the producers, writers and sponsors of that evil movie. It just openly displayed abomination before God and drew its viewers into more acts of abuse and misdeeds. We, as the church, have ignored this evil for too long. I, for one, refuse to handle the enemy with kid gloves any longer because our Christian voice should be the strongest voice. It is mandatory to use the Bible as the standard for our voice. We must expose evil and immoral behavior, and then label it exactly for what it is.

The sports arena is not immune to the influence of immorality either as my pastor pointed out when Robert Griffin III was told to turn his T-shirt inside out so that the message "GOT JESUS" would not be seen during his interview. On the other hand, the sports networks proudly displayed the kiss of the gay NFL draft pick for the Rams and his partner over and over like it was a proud moment for all Americans. Christians should have united and protested that like it was a crime and a shame because it was to God and should have been to us.

Ten years later, the music and music videos have become far worse, full of kinky behavior and aberration. Many black singers and writers continue to use the word N_ _ _ _ E R in their songs like a badge of honor. Much of the music in every genre encourages same gender sex, multiple partner sex, and narcissistic sex as though it is as ordinary an occurrence as trying a new flavor of ice cream. Ten years later, everything has gotten far worse through more sexual anomaly and violence. The sex-traffic trade that is fully on the radar now is the best proof of how badly and deviant sexual sins have become. Ten years ago, Sue and I shared multiple examples of how sin was running rampant in so many ways. Now, things are much worse and many people, including believers, choose to exhibit an ungodly lifestyle like it's simply a popular fad. The few shows mentioned earlier are a mere representation of what movies, TV, commercials, and music display as normal which confuses both youth and adults alike, which I totally understand.

Furthermore, God's word says that marriage is honorable. The marriage bed is to be treated with love and respect. Two men or two women having sex cannot reproduce and honor God. A man or woman who has sex with someone other than his/her spouse can bring disease or outside children into their marriage and this does not honor God. People sleeping with animals will breed disease, and grown people having sex with children cause damage to that child for life. None of these perverted sexual acts honor God. Anyone who practices such acts needs to stop. Anyone who thinks he or she can continue to practice such sinful behavior and not have consequences or not be held accountable to God is lying to himself. Right and wrong are true and absolute concepts. If you do not believe this, SHAME ON YOU!

"Every way of a man is right in his own eyes, but the Lord weighs the heart." (Prov. 21:2—Modern English Translation)

While we slept, satan has tried to take full dominion over what God has given to us. We must now choose to unite on a greater scale. Together, the weight of all of our voices will help tip the scales and call people back to God, just like it did in Biblical times. When John the Baptist was born, there was a dynamic prophetic voice on the rise who would one day say, "Prepare the way for the Lord." Our united prophetic voice can lead the remnant of people who are willing to take a stand right now. There is an army rising up over the horizon to break down every stronghold and chain for God and for His Glory. Please, it is time to wake up and render your voice along with ours. Now is our time to be heard, and united we will stand.

"Except the LORD build the house, they labor in vain that built it: except the LORD keep the city, the watchman wakes but in vain."—Psalm 127:1

Sue's Voice:

It is very revealing to go back and reread what Deidre and I wrote in this chapter ten years ago. In 2004 the handwriting was on the wall, and now in 2014, the results of what we were beginning to see then are indeed evident. It seems that anything goes in modern society and public schools except anything from a Christian viewpoint. Our school systems teach inclusion for Islam, Buddhism, etc. but threaten suspension for an elementary student who brought his Bible story-book to school for free reading time. Reality television programs show anything and everything from *Bridezilla* and *Big Brother* to *Honey Boo Boo* and *Dance Moms* with all manner of foul language, selfish behavior, and a "me first" mentality, but questioned the *Duck Dynasty* Robertson family's use of prayer in every episode. We have more cable channels available than ever before, and many evenings there is NOTHING TO WATCH except junk! Shame on all involved—what we feared has come to pass—everything is acceptable, and if you object, you are a hater and in need of reform. For example, NFL players now have to take inclusion or rehabilitation classes when they speak out or joke about the gay lifestyle. However, a Christian husband and wife minister team in Idaho is threatened with arrest and big fines for choosing not to marry a gay couple at their Hitching Post chapel. The Bill of Rights guarantees of freedom of speech and religion seem to be diminishing rapidly in this country.

The American public apparently accepts many of the ongoing changes as evidenced by two states—Washington and Colorado—voting in 2012 to sell marijuana for recreational use, with the profits already generating millions of dollars. This past week, I heard ESPN report that New Jersey wants to allow wagering on NFL games which the league is fighting. Is anyone else noticing the direction all this is going and questioning when the world turned upside down besides me?

I have several friends on Facebook who post pro-gay articles occasionally and when anyone responds with "anti" remarks, the majority go after them with comments such as, "You're sick," "You're the one with the problem," or "Haters never win." The Hollywood agenda has succeeded, and we now have a generation who was raised with TV and movie role models who are gay or support the gay lifestyle. Sometimes it's exhausting to keep fighting against the storm or attempt to roll that stone up the mountain, but it's what those of us who hold to our beliefs have to do. We can't give up, whether it's on social media, at the ballot box, or discussion forums. I can only speak for myself, but I'm not a hater, although I will seriously have to work on that statement when it concerns groups like Isis. Don't I have a right to my opinions and beliefs, or are the only ones that count those of the Liberal/leftist leaning groups?

In reading Deidre's TYL, I felt like a voyeur watching a forbidden scene. I was reminded how we in the Christian community have failed our Lord and our civilization! It started slowly, but surely moved along without most of us even realizing it. I remember when I was in transition from elementary to middle school in 1959, the huge hit *Bonanza* was introduced on TV on Sunday night. Some in my church complained that they had to choose whether to attend evening services or watch that family program. Move onto my state's repeal of the Blue laws a few years later. These laws, known also as Sunday laws, were designed to restrict or ban some or all Sunday activities for religious standards. They restricted the sale of most items on this day that used to be known as the Lord's Day. After the repeal, the mall was open as were grocery stores, gas stations, drug stores—it was just another retail day. In 1975, NBC, the network that had introduced *Bonanza*, started showcasing *Saturday Night Live* and in 1980 a new network BET was founded, followed closely by MTV the following year. Can you see the progression? At every milestone, most churches and congregations remained silent, sleeping and slumbering as Deidre described. We will never know how long the family-acceptable standards would have remained had Christians united to complain about language, sarcastic skits which ridiculed family standards, sexual situations, lyrics, and dress. If we had put racial separation and denominational differences aside, we could have made a noticeable difference. Today, due to social media, I know many people who attend their religious services on Sunday morning, then look forward to watching some of the very programs Deidre mentioned in her update. Our standards have been affected as well, and I need to include myself in this analysis. If we call ourselves Christians, we need to act like it.

I see where we have gone in ten years. I watch the youngsters coming up in our extended families and see precious babies being born to church couples. What is the world going to be like for them in a few years? It's a frightening thought! Those groups we mentioned in our original *Shame On You* chapter remain vigilant. They continue to work to remove all mention of God or religion from the public sphere, design revealing clothing, provide movies and TV programming that use all manner of profanity and sexual situations, and record lyrics and videos that are questionable—need I mention "twerking?" Are we willing to fight for more acceptable things which will positively impact the future of our children? I hope so.

"A lie doesn't become truth, wrong doesn't become right, and evil doesn't become good, just because it's accepted by a majority."
—Rick Warren

CHAPTER XII

People in the Middle

*"Who knows but that you were placed here for
such a time as this."*
—Esther 4:14

Voice I:

"The people in the middle" is a phrase that refers to those people who are concerned with accomplishing their God-ordained purpose in life. It is my opinion that these people are not concerned about race, denomination, or the special rights of any one particular group of people. The focus of PIMs (People in the Middle) is the well-being of others. This group realizes that we must invest in our youth today in order that they might become an asset tomorrow. They believe that children are one of our greatest human resources and that we need to protect them as never before. PIMs are mindful of the examples we set before them as teachers, leaders, lay people, and parents, realizing that personal prejudices and immoral behavior can be carefully taught by one generation to another. PIMs can be found as the leaders of Boy Scouts, little league teams, after-school tutors, medical workers, and dance instructors. No doubt the coach in the movie, "Sandlot," learned to be a PIM before it was all said and done!

PIMs know that all people are unique and different, but that our differences don't matter in the overall picture. We should be the "light of the world" and the "salt of the earth." We come from all walks of life, nationalities, and races. We are the ones from every area that look outside of ourselves to try to understand others. However, today there are those people who would try to persuade you to see others in a different, more negative way.

Louis Farrakhan was once quoted in a *Time* magazine issue as being the "voice of Black America." I was angered by this and vehemently told Sue that, "he does not speak for me!" As a well-known leader of American Muslims, he once called God's chosen people—the Jews— "the devil" and actively promotes dissension between the black and white races. Likewise, I'm sure many white people have been ashamed of David Duke and other white supremacists or Middle Easterners of the evil terrorist acts of Osama bin Laden.

I say that the people in the middle are not like these individuals. They want to get along with and understand other races. PIMs have to speak out against racial inequalities and injustices. They feel that they must help our children to learn that we are all interconnected, and what one group does can and has hurt others. For example, the jail systems in America may be overcrowded with a majority of black men, but every race of people helps maintain and pay for the upkeep of these "bad boys" of society. Likewise if more people are not inter-ested or involved in our current public education system, the produc-tivity of the students, those future tax-paying citizens, could affect their retirement funds.

It is time for those of us who really care for others to realize that we are our "brothers' keepers." It is time for us—the people in the mid-dle—to rise and set aside racial, denominational, and cultural differ-ences and see the greater work—to preserve, prepare, and propel our youth to succeed.

We must accept the realities of life and openly use what we know to solve our societal demons. We can no longer push them under the carpet with the old, worn-out excuses that "It's always been this way and won't ever change." The call to the occasion is now, and it is to the people in the middle, the ones who believe that they can make a difference right where they are for the bigger picture.

Here are some realities that, I believe, we need to face in order to move forward:

—Cultural differences do exist.
—We must use the knowledge of these cultural differences to help improve our schools, work places, communities, and churches.
—Not every child can or will go to college.
—Each individual must be expected to contribute to society, not just receive from it.
—We are in the 21st Century and our educational system must be also.

People in the middle—I know you're out there in every community, city, and state. I want to encourage you to get involved somewhere, even if it's just in one place with one person. Remember, tomorrow may never come for you, so what better thing could you do today than to make a difference, right where you are?

> "One person can make a difference
> and every person should try."
> —John F. Kennedy

Voice II:

In our society today, those on the left and those on the right are often heard debating issues on news programs, talking to famous interviewers like Oprah Winfrey, Larry King, and Bill O'Reilly, and writing best-selling books. The majority of us will never be interviewed because we are somewhere in the middle of these opinions, and our voices are rarely heard on television or elsewhere. That is why Deidre decided to write this book and graciously asked me to participate with her so that the "still, small voices" of those in the middle could be heard.

Those of us who are working hard all week at jobs that support our families have little time left over to become involved in the dialogue over government, political candidates, new laws, educational reforms, religious liberty, and other varying types of issues. We are the ones who support this nation, taxed to the max and trying to make sense of all the talk from those supporting the conservative, independent, and liberal agendas. We are quietly coaching recreational teams for our children, taking to the mountains or the seashores for brief family vacations, and trying to instill our values and beliefs to our children through church, scouting, music lessons, and other activities. Life is very complicated and seems to be getting even more demanding than it was in the late 60s and early 70s when I began raising children. Voices are clamoring at us from every side, leaving very little time for us to withdraw and analyze what is best for ourselves and those we love. Spokespersons for the special interest groups get the publicity while ordinary people like your neighbor who mows your grass or bakes lasagna for your family when you are hospitalized is ignored.

This country was built with the "blood, sweat, and tears" of these types of people who thought of others first and themselves later. They worked and sacrificed so their children could have a better life in a country which valued freedom and morality over all else, believing that given an opportunity, most people would benefit from such a society. They fought in wars to defend the freedoms our Founding Fathers wrote in two very important documents: The Declaration of Independence and the Constitution of the United States. However, today many people don't seem to realize that the first document says in plain English that we were given unalienable rights—life, liberty, and the pursuit of happiness—by our Creator, while the other outlines our plan of government and adds additional rights and laws to benefit all citizens. Some of these same people who don't understand these documents would question the validity of our Pledge of Allegiance mentioning a "God" and try to defend their stance by quoting the first amendment "separation of church and state," which was written in a time not far removed from a monarch dictating how the citizenry would believe. This nation, which was founded on a belief in God, is in danger of eliminating Him from public life by those who may never have even known Him.

The irony of this situation is that the very people who would be so hurt and mortified by such judicial rulings or laws often refrain from speaking out publicly about their outrage. They seem to believe that there is nothing they can do to change the course of events because, I think, they feel that their comments or feelings just don't matter. However, those who would take their religious rights away from them have no problem speaking out and spouting off to any camera or interviewer who will listen.

I fear that some of these people in the middle don't even vote in most elections, feeling that their vote wouldn't make any difference. They are unaware that, historically, one vote has made a dramatic difference in many world-wide political decisions. For example, it has been said that Adolf Hitler was placed in control of Germany's Nazi Party in 1921 by just one vote. Perhaps if he had not held that high ranking position, he would not have been elected Chancellor of that country in 1933, and over sixty million people would not have lost their lives in World War II. If that awesome thought doesn't change your mind about voting, consider that in 1960, Senator John F. Kennedy of Massachusetts won the 1960 Presidential election by the astonishing margin of less than two votes per voting precinct. That small margin gave him the necessary electoral votes to narrowly defeat Vice President Richard Nixon and become our 35th President.

My portion of this chapter is a bit difference in concept than Deidre's and is dedicated to the hope that I can awaken in these types of people the reality of how important they really are to the democratic process in this country. I want to encourage the PIMs to let their voice be heard more often than it is now. Look in the mirror: You are an American-born or naturalized citizen with many rights guaranteed. You have the same freedom as the ACLU to speak out, peacefully meet and demonstrate for what you think is important, write your Congressmen or women, and more importantly, vote in every election. As I told Deidre (see Ch. I), voting is one of your most important rights as well as a responsibility of citizenship in this country. We are a Democratic Republic, which means the power to govern the United States of America comes from the people through their elected representatives.

The voting record of the American public is dismally low. Consider this: Even in Presidential elections, almost half of the registered voters in this country don't bother to fulfill their responsibility as citizens and vote. Candidates know this and often rely on and listen to the special interest groups and those people who can be counted upon to show up at the polls and vote so they can win the election. Every vote counts today as much as it did in 1921 and 1960, as the 2000 election between George W. Bush and Al Gore demonstrated.

Several years ago, former President, Ronald Reagan, referred to you—"the people in the middle"—as the Silent Majority, and his speeches seemed to rally many who otherwise wouldn't have become involved

in political campaigns and volunteer work to an activism that bene-
fited many people, communities, and organizations. Today you can
make your voice heard in your community in a variety of ways. Carefully monitor what your elected or appointed school board is doing.
Consider their decisions and if you agree or disagree with their focus,
let them know it. Volunteer to help in your local schools or with the
parks and recreation departments in your locality. Stand for positive
changes in your home town and hold your elected officials—local,
state, and national—responsible for their actions.

Apathy and the "busyness" of daily life can seem to sap the strength
from our country, community by community. People are so busy
making a living that they count on those people whose business it is
to govern to simply do their jobs. But who's "minding the store" and
actually watching to ensure that things are being done as they should
be? It might be that you—the parents of school-aged children, the
retired grandparents, the social club member who enlists the mem-
bership in a community project, and others—are the ones who can
truly make a lasting difference if only you get involved and try!

Today, more than ever, we need people who are willing to speak out
against those things they believe are wrong and lead their friends and
neighbors in actions to remedy problems that need fixing. All it ever
takes are a few individuals who are willing to step out and lead the
way. Are you willing to be such a person? If so, you can help to make
positive changes for your neighborhood, your city, perhaps your state,
and even your nation. More importantly, you will be a role model for
your children and others around you. Remember, you might have
been placed in your little area of the world, right now, "for such a time
as this!"

"Be the change that you want."
—Ghandi

TWO VOICES AS ONE…FOR YOU

People in the middle might be here because it is their time. This is the time for them to step up and step out to make a difference that will last a lifetime and beyond. It is important for you to realize that what you accept in this life—immorality that calls itself "choice," lifestyle situations that mock a Holy and Righteous God, language and behavior that negatively impact your children—you teach to everyone around you. The choices you make affect your life and the lives of those you touch because God often uses ordinary people to accomplish His extraordinary plans. Indeed we are but "small voices for such a time as this," but a small voice can transform a life or a situation just as one small candle can illuminate a darkened room. We encourage you to let your voice be heard!

TEN YEARS LATER

Deidre's Voice:

It is quite amazing, though not incredulous, how much things can and have changed within a ten year time frame. Ten years ago, I defined People in the Middle or PIMs as those individuals who are the unsung heroes including, but certainly not limited to, school teachers/counselors, the Little League coaches of Pop Warner, the Girl Scout/Boy Scout leaders, medical workers, and piano, dance and music instructors. These people sacrifice their time and money to help develop youth all across America on a daily basis with little to no recognition. Of course, true PIMs don't want recognition; they do what they do because of an inner ignition switch placed there by God, our Creator. That fire was established deep within the hearts of each and every PIM in order to fulfill that purpose for which they were designed. In our original chapter, I referenced how extremists in our country are very outspoken, trying to be the prominent voice for America, and far too many times succeeding. Now there are no longer a *few evil* extreme voices out there with the agenda of dividing or silencing People in the Middle, but there is *an entire coalition of evil* voices who are the close kin of Osama bin Laden; those people are known as ISIS/ISIL. When ISIS beheaded an American aid worker, Peter Kassig, on November 17, 2014, President Obama said that "it was an act of pure evil." The use of those two seemingly contradictory terms unequivocally stresses how full of evil ISIL really is. Yet, it rings with a bit of irony when I consider that this distorted and evil group sincerely believes they are actually cleansing their country of infidels through the executions of foreigners.

I also previously mentioned some realities that needed to be faced in order to bridge some gaps and give PIMs a more united voice (Ch. XII). One of those stated realities was "Not every child can or will go to college." When former New York City Mayor and billionaire, Michael Bloomberg, gave it as advice for high school seniors, the media went into frenzy. Mr. Bloomberg said, "Forget college, become a plumber instead." (New York; CNN Money) Of course, his main point was that college is just becoming too expensive for some individuals who have skills and talents upon leaving high school. With training they could begin earning money right away instead of going into a stupendous amount of debt and possibly spending the rest of their lives repaying college loans. Perhaps many PIMs would agree with Mr. Bloomberg, but those who work with children already know college is not for every child because we have spent time with these precious commodities, and we understand what the rest of society may never know. This is that every individual has a specific purpose. The Bible already said it best in Jeremiah 1:5, "Before I formed you in your mother's womb, I already had a purpose for you. " God already designed us with gifts, talents and a purpose. If we would just encourage our children to discover that purpose, it would save us all a lot of time, pain and cash! God's way is always the best way.

Today, I would clearly assert that the PIMs are probably a majority of those who identify themselves as Christians. We are caught "dead-smack" in the middle of where pure evil inevitably prevails, and thinking perhaps there is no "real" evil. Now more than ever, Christians are in the middle being crushed between the atmospheric pressures of right and wrong, constantly having to choose a side on an almost daily basis. No longer is Christianity receiving the attention it once did as the epitome of the true successful lifestyle. There was a time in our history when art, music, education, and family were based around the Christian principals. Much like a first-born child, Christianity received all of the attention; being totally pampered, treasured, and coddled like the baby child of the average family. People chose to respect the church and the mention of God. Even though they may have disliked the church and what it stood for, individuals still showed Christians and the House of God some type of admiration. Many non-Christians would not even curse or dare to drink alcohol in front of a church. Now anything goes, both inside and outside of the House of God. Cute phrases like What Would Jesus Do? (WWJD) and the little fish signs were highly accepted and publicized by many who were saved and unsaved alike. People used to embrace morality, but today's standards of living do not seem to reflect it any more.

Today, Christians find themselves so much in the middle that they are exemplifying symptoms of a "middle child!" Like a lot of children in the middle, they are often times overlooked. Christians are excluded on purpose and neglected with an air of finality by not even being considered by the vast majority. No one cares that you have a belief system based on the principals and standards of the Holy Bible. A lot of Christians are professing the faith by words only and simply going through the motions of attending church on Sunday. Many feel that no one is watching them, so they don't want to be a Godly example any longer, and have cast off restraint, going about and "doing their own thing."

It is in the middle where we are currently being squeezed to death. I believe Christians are the true PIMs of today and have to redefine themselves based on God's word and not society's expectations. As the People in the Middle, we have to get our voice, influence, and power back. Do you desire to voice any suggestions? We're listening . . .

Sue's Voice:

Oh, PIMs how much we still need you today! But when I think about it, I <u>have</u> seen some of you, hard at work in volunteer organizations throughout my small retirement town in WV. From the Humane Society to the Veterans' posts and organizations, you are out there making a difference. I know how hard my church and other area groups work with food pantries, plan community work days to benefit the elderly, help build homes for families through Habitat For Humanity, plan and fill weekend food packages for underprivileged children to take home for the weekends, and gather to clean up litter by the roadsides and along our Ohio River waterway. I'm sure the list could continue, but you know what I mean. I wonder how much more we could do if more of us were involved?

I remember how Deidre and I designed a narrow bookmark to hand out at book signings that had our *Small Voices* cover on it and the following words:

> Be a PIM. "People in the Middle" make a difference
> where they are right now! Speak out!
> Vote! Stand for right! Be a light!

Are these words simply idealistic ramblings, or would the world, indeed, be a better place for us all if we ascribed to this life philosophy? I know I would rather live here in this "new and improved" world, so I will continue to encourage you to follow those bookmark hints. I definitely found a PIM recently in a small article in the *Parade* magazine of my local Sunday newspaper which was headlined "Acts of Kindness." In it, Alex Radelch, a 21-yr-old Purdue student, was quoted as wondering, "What would happen if kindness became normal?" To find out he decided to travel across the country and perform "acts of random kindness" which he called ARKS. This young man started a worldwide movement, the ARK project Now, (arkproject-now.com) and says, "Every act of kindness can change someone's life." I guess we PIMS could join the ARKs because our philosophies mesh so well.

Since my section of our original "*Voices*" concentrated mainly on historical documents and encouraged citizen voter participation, I find it interesting that ten years later as I write this update, we have just completed the 2014 mid-term elections where a near-record low of 36.3% of registered voters cast their ballots. This turnout was the lowest since 1942, resembling turnouts from the Great Depression and the start of World War II. Since the right to vote is a fundamental right and responsibility in any democracy, it strikes me as a pitiful shame that so few people are taking advantage of it.

In talking with family and neighbors, I understand the reasons. Politicians are not trusted and few people see a difference between the two parties. Why vote—you're going to get the same result regardless of who occupies the White House or sits in Congress? The futility of this situation and the perceived impression of the dysfunction of our government leads to the low voter turnout.

However, what really worries me is the seemingly "dumbing down" of our population. When you ask specific questions that any knowledgeable person should know, it's amazing how few answers you get, regardless of age and ethnicity. It seems that many people are so consumed with their daily schedules or have their faces so consistently stuck in their hand-held devices, that they are news ignorant on many occasions. I am absolutely astounded at the interviews I occasionally watch on the Bill O'Reilly show called "Watters World." In these four to five minute segments, reporter Jesse Watters goes to college campuses, shopping malls, sports events, just "out and about," asking basic questions about our elected leaders, the location of different states or countries, when Christopher Columbus sailed, etc., and the answers or lack of them are astounding. I know I taught the answers. I'm not throwing stones at the teachers for this lack of knowledge, because you have to have a useable, willing slate on which to write facts. People just don't seem to care anymore! That kind of apathy is going to harm us, figuratively and literally! For example, today's news headlines involves MIT professor, Jonathan Gruber, known as the architect of the Affordable Health Care Act (Obamacare) characterizing the American voter as "stupid," and explaining how the administration pushed through this health care legislation by not telling the truth about the law. When opposition did surface, few people did any research, major networks failed to report discrepancies, and no one paid any attention. Apathy can be dangerous!

This is our country, filled with cities, towns, and neighborhoods that need our attention and interest. People in the middle can make a huge difference for everyone within their circle of influence. Many people talk about Karma—that "what goes around, comes around." One day we will be the ones who need help from others. It starts with you—pay it forward now!

CHAPTER XIII

Teachers Are People Too!

"Be kind; for everyone you meet is fighting a hard battle."
—*Rev. John Watson*

Voice I:

A lifeline is someone who reaches out and helps you when you need it the most. Sue is one of my lifelines because during a dark period in my life, she kept me going and literally saved my teaching career. One year, when I was involved in a series of car accidents and slipped into depression, Sue was there to help keep me focused. She would bring me news of how the students were doing, class sets of "Get Well Soon" cards, and posters that I could hang in my room when I returned to school. It was during this time in my life that I felt like giving up on everything, and then God would send her my way to offer me a ray of hope and one more reason to "hang in there." I remember that Larry, my husband of fourteen years, was often away from home during this time due to his Navy career. Although he was involved and very supportive, he was not there. Again, it was Sue, who helped me with our two children, Shamona and Larry, Jr. Experiencing all the pain from the car accidents and the pressures of being mom and dad with Larry away, it was hard for me to even think about facing one hundred or more students every day in my mental state. However, Sue was there to remind me of the many faith statements I had so often quoted to her when her youngest son, Bryan, had been diagnosed with diabetes. Now she was giving the Word back to me, and I had to accept it and move on with my life, despite all the challenges. Later, after my ordeals, Sue went through several trials of her own, but the greatest had to be the loss of this son, when he went into a diabetic coma and died. I was so lost for words and how to comfort her, but I remembered how God's Word had helped me to heal and I knew it would be the only thing to help Sue as well.

Bryan was a well-built, good looking young man with gorgeous auburn hair that would put many women to shame. I remember a statement he once made to Sue that we laughed about on several occasions. Bryan had visited the school one day to see his mom when our worst class in several years was coming back from lunch. Filled with lots of sugar and playfulness, their behavior left a lot to be desired as they entered Sue's room that day. With a smirk on his face, he remarked to his mom, "The natives are restless today!" All I could do was laugh and agree despite my embarrassment because our African-American students were really misbehaving that day. Even if I had wanted to feel angry, how could I dispute what he had said? I did wonder why Bryan had to see something like that because he was one of Sue's family who had experienced several negative encounters with Blacks. She was trying to encourage him to look for the positives in everyone, regardless of race and then he had to see the perfect representation of negativity in those students. I told Sue I would love to have an opportunity to see Bryan personally to share and encourage him with a more positive perspective. Fortunately before he died, we did get to share with one another several times. After his death, I was able to go on a Walk for Diabetes with Sue in his memory, and I treasure all of those memories.

Sue was in the delivery room when my youngest child was born. I remember telling her months earlier that we were "claiming" a boy. Although this term was a relatively new word for Sue, once I showed her the Scriptural basis for it, she readily grasped this concept and brought me the cutest little blue rattle with teddy bears, sailors and boats on it. We laughed and contemplated the name Emmanuel (God with us), then rejoiced when the doctor confirmed that the baby was a boy! From that moment on, I knew Sue and Richard would be the perfect Godparents—and they are.

Somehow through it all, we managed to survive, day by day. No matter how others view us – as the answer to all the questions, the cause of all the trouble at school, or a temporary fix for a deep-rooted problem—we are still people with individual lives and many needs of our own. I have often had to tell my students when they are misbehaving, "Look, I am someone's mother, someone's wife, and loved by many—you will not treat me this way!" I go on to ask them, "Would you act like this if your mother were here? Imagine I'm your mother." These questions have been effective for many, but not for all. No, I'm not their mother, but I have had to mother students, not as a conscious effort but as the situation arises because it is a natural reaction for me. Once when a student confided in her journal entry that she was being molested and threatened by a close relative, I comforted her with the words, "God will take care of you, but you must tell." Even though I was reprimanded in writing by my principal because a police officer overheard the conversation, I knew I had done the right thing. What was in me—my Christian faith—naturally came out when it was needed. I told my principal that I would try not to mention God at school, but I couldn't promise that it wouldn't happen again. This was because even though I was a teacher in a public school, I was at heart a child of God who naturally spoke of Him. I compared it this way: "You wouldn't tell a dog that he can't bark, so don't tell me not to talk about God."

I remember my first year at Davis Middle School, when I told my students to sit quietly while I went to the restroom. Those eighth graders looked at me in utter amazement and I could only respond, "Yes, I have to do that too!" They burst out in laughter as I quickly made my exit, and chuckled as I thought, "They really don't see me as a person."

Teachers wear many hats, and I am a person with many roles. I am a woman, God's minister, a wife, a mother, a daughter, a sister, a teacher, a colleague, a friend, and an acquaintance. To view me as only a teacher is to miss so many other valuable parts because I am a person, just like you.

Voice II:

Every day untold numbers of people leave home in the morning and drive, walk, or car pool to work. Many of them carry their lunches, a bag full of paperwork, pens, books, and perhaps a laptop computer with them as they enter a building, find their key, and open a door which leads to another world. This world contains many seats, a few tables, a variety of supplies, a chalk or dry erase board, and a bulletin board. These people are teachers and within their classroom, they affect their little corner of the world in many ways. However, most of their students have never thought or don't even care that the person whose name is above the door of this room is a person with the same needs, wants, and dreams as everyone else in their domain. Rarely does the thought come to the minds of some administrators, parents, and students that "teachers are people too!"

Every day teachers go to work, leaving behind challenges, struggles, heartache, and who knows what else to greet other people's children and attempt to teach them something new. Daily, all kinds of paperwork needs to be completed, lesson plans designed, phone calls made or returned, classrooms of students managed, and curriculum taught with enthusiasm and energy. Deep within, their hearts may be breaking over a failed marriage, a wayward child, a court decision, upcoming surgery for themselves or a loved one, the military deployment of a spouse, the possibility of nursing home care for a parent, or a myriad of other issues that threaten to topple their sanity. But all anyone ever sees is Mr. Austin or Mrs. Bell unlocking that door, beginning another day, and trying to put a smile on his or her face. Our public needs to know and understand that we were people before we became teachers, and people we remain.

One of the most amusing aspects of this job is meeting students as you go about your daily life after school or on the weekends. Shortly after I began my teaching career in middle school, I was shopping for groceries at a nearby store, and encountered one of my students and her parent in one of the aisles. You would have thought the child, who was accustomed to seeing me teach her history or reading, would faint from the shock at seeing me in a "regular" part of the world, outside the walls of the school. Of all things, I was dressed in jeans and a sweatshirt! This situation has multiplied itself many times and I never cease to be amused at the reaction of students when they see me in the "real" world. Most are pleased and want to introduce me to a parent or sibling, but some seem to have never thought that I'm a person just like them who needs food, gasoline, or maybe some Tylenol!

I have worked with many teachers who have gone through difficult, challenging days while attempting to continue to teach the students who were under their supervision. While I tried to remain sympathetic, supportive, and compassionate, I never truly understood what they were going through until a two to three year period when I felt like the Biblical character, Job, as one challenging situation after another befell me. During this time, I lived through serious problems with my grown children over which I had absolutely no control and the untimely death of my youngest son at age 28 from diabetic complications. Then a lump appeared on my neck that needed two needle biopsies for a (blessed) benign diagnosis, and uterine fibroids plagued me for months before ultimately beginning to hemorrhage while I was trying to teach my last class one October day. When this problem required major surgery, I did what I had done during the entire challenging period, and held fast to the promise that God would not give me more than He and I could handle together. I continued to teach my students, unlocking that door every morning except for the twenty-one days plus Christmas vacation when I was absent for surgical leave. I dealt with my problems when I had to, but welcomed the diversion of teaching 128 students during the week to momentarily take my mind away from the heart-breaking drama that was happening with my family and within my body. I was definitely a teacher, but so much more a person with all the troubles I was struggling to overcome.

Teachers are like everyone else—the cashier at the grocery store, the mechanic at the car dealership, or your beautician down the road—living through the good times and the bad, just doing the best they can. Their daily job description might be different because they interact with children and specific curriculum every day instead of money, spark plugs, or curling irons. But they can have families that need them, sick children at home, or a spouse with problems that interferes with their ability to focus solely on the problems individual students have within their classes. Your child is an important part of their life this year, but because this teacher—this person—has wants and needs of his/her own, individual students cannot be the only focus of his/her life.

So the next time you walk into your neighborhood school for a parent-teacher conference or when you feel the need to pick up the phone and call your child's teacher, please remember that the individual speaking to you is a person who may be facing challenging situations in their own life. He/she should be willing to meet you more than halfway in working with your student, but they don't need personal attacks, impatience, or preconceived notion of incompetence or worse still, prejudice. Work with them to help your child, and always remember that just like you, "teachers are people too."

TWO VOICES AS ONE…FOR YOU

An old Indian story ends with the proverb that "to understand another, you must walk a mile in his moccasins." That advice could apply to this chapter because we have tried to describe the daily walk that teachers take during their careers. Both of us agree that many people fail to see teachers as the people they are. We are professionals who have so many daily and long-term responsibilities that it almost seems unfair for life to throw illness, family problems, and additional challenges our way. However, it happens all the time to many educators, and when it does, teachers do the best they know how to do in what may be very difficult circumstances. While they have chosen a career in which they work with children or young people, adults, computers, deadlines, and curriculum they also have to fulfill the other roles that life has handed them—those of wife/husband, mother/father, child, sibling, church member, and neighbor, among others. Please remember that most days their plate is very full. Nevertheless, many teachers try to remain positive and upbeat while teaching yet another concept to another class filled with your children. We are people, with all the frailties you may see when you look in the mirror, but not everyone realizes that. Now you do!

> "TEACHING—You laugh, you cry, and you work harder than you ever thought you could. Some days you're trying to change the world and some days you're just trying to

make it through the day. Your wallet is empty, your heart
is full, and your mind is packed with memories of kids
who have changed your life. Just another day in the
classroom."—Krissy Venosdale

TEN YEARS LATER

Deidre's Voice:

Recently I met a young man whom I came to highly respect in just a
short amount of time. This individual enriched my life tremendously
as he began to share his life's experiences with a group of high school
students. While he expounded on his own personal testimony, he told
this particular group how God had placed key adults and college professors in his life who granted him so much unmerited favor that it
impacted his life in ways he never thought possible. He told them it
was mainly because he made the conscious decision to recognize and
honor those teachers first, and they, in return, displayed deference
towards him. Likewise, he further encouraged the students to place
high value on the leaders and instructors God has placed in their lives
that help mold and shape them into better people. There was no
doubt in my mind that he must have fully understood how "teachers
are people too."

Throughout his presentation, he made several profound statements
including, "Cater to the needs of the people who you need." He also
told the students, "If I change my surroundings, I change who is
around me." Both of those statements spoke to the person and teacher
within me simultaneously. Since publishing the first edition of our
book, I have more completely lived out that first statement by learning to love and enjoy how to serve those whom I need. In other words,
I can acknowledge with confidence that God has assigned me to serve

and cater to young people. Many young people can and do benefit from the gifts and talents given to me by God. However, most importantly, it is around young people where I feel my greatest sense of joy, purpose, and fulfillment.

Over the past ten years, I have learned more fully how to balance being a woman of God, a wife, a mother, a teacher, a friend, and a minister as I continued working on my assignments with young people. However, it was while performing my responsibilities as the administrator and lead-teacher at True Gospel Ministries Christian Academy located in Suffolk, Virginia, that I learned the most. This time of learning began in 1999, shortly after the infamous Columbine shootings, when I submitted my resignation to Hampton Public Schools. I had previously taught school in Charlotte, NC, Killeen, TX and Newport News, VA, but Hampton is where I had the longest teaching period of ten years. It is where I had met Sue, where we had experienced the loss of our first student, and where I was well-liked and respected as an educator and colleague. Furthermore, I had tenure and a comfortable position as the Literary Passport Test (LPT) Specialist in the area of writing. That meant I had gone from having over 120 students per day to classes of ten or less. Needless to say, I was comfortable when God began to prick my heart about leaving the public school system.

One of the most difficult topics to discuss with others is hearing the voice of God. As Christians, we are to continue to practice how to hear God more clearly. I have never heard God speak to me audibly, but He does speak to me through His written word. At this time, I began to experience an almost non-stop tugging at my heart to begin a Christian school. To make sure this idea was from God, I also asked for two but received confirmations from three different people that the time had come for me to make this incredible move of faith. At the core, God made it clear to me based on His word in Deuteronomy 6:7 where He commands His people to talk and teach the children about Him as they sit, walk, lie down, and rise up daily. Only a solid Christian environment would allow for an excellent balance of academics and a love for the knowledge of God.

My first struggle was a sense of embarrassment and at times, fear, as several of my colleagues expressed surprise that I would leave a tenured job with decent pay and good benefits in order to begin a Christian school from scratch! The decision to resign from my cozy position was probably the most difficult decision I have had to make in my entire life. The next and larger struggle was telling my husband because we had just recently purchased a beautiful tri-level home in Hampton, VA, a brand new Mark IV Chevrolet van, and some stunning Queen Anne furniture. Now I was telling Larry that God was speaking to me about stopping work at a steady job with a good income to begin a new job with little to no income and no benefits. What could I possibly say to lessen the impact of the unspoken truth that our two-income home was about to become a household dependent on only his earnings. I knew full well even before I approached him that we had based our decision to make those major purchases based on the fact that we had two reliable incomes. Of course, I blamed it all on God. "No way that is happening, Dee!" exclaimed my husband. "Are you sure that is God speaking to you or are those your own thoughts?" My greatest argument was that I had recently asked him if I could take a two-year leave of absence from my job in order to complete Graduate school, but he had told me to wait for about three years. Now it seemed that God had other plans for me, but I had to wait until God spoke directly to Larry's heart also.

A few days before the Columbine shooting, God spoke gently to my husband, and told him that this new generation of children was simply not being taught about Him on a daily basis. Even much worse than that, so many children were being brought up without hearing about God at all. I still have the sweetest e-mail Larry sent to me while he was out to sea stating how he would cover the family financially while I obeyed God's command. Today, this testimony consistently remains as I remember how he and God paid every bill without any disconnects, repossessions, or foreclosures. The money he made was never enough to pay every bill, but God somehow allowed him to make it all work together.

Once I felt free to begin the Christian school, God really blessed us with furniture, rugs, supplies and food. The alternative school I was leaving had also housed a pre-school program that was ending. God blessed our school to receive all of their furniture and a lot of supplies as well when He gave me the nerve to tell the school administrator about our need. I was also emboldened to ask a stranger in a store for some carpet as a donation, and he said, "Yes!" I could not believe how God was providing, but He was teaching me how provision is always made available for any vision He gives us.

Even though I was being obedient to God's instruction, the first year the school opened seemed almost unbearable. My children and I had to wake up at 4:00 am each morning in order for us to leave Hampton by 5:00 am, and then arrive in Suffolk to open the school/day care by 6:00 am because God had instructed me to begin the school with children ages two through four, day care was a vital part of the school. I had to be strong for both of our children, especially our daughter, who struggled with adjusting because our new location was in a different socio-economic area from what she was used to in Hampton. Some of the children in her fifth grade class teased her terribly, telling her daily that she talked and acted "white." I had to get our daughter counseling, and found a support group for myself as well called

Mother's in Touch (MIT). Our son was in kindergarten and adjusted well, but he missed his own room and toys. They both had to catch the school bus after school to a friend's house and wait for me to pick them up at the end of daycare which was after 6:00 pm. I did have additional support with the school, but no one could help open or close that first year. On the evenings when we had scheduled church services, it would be well after 10:00 pm before we would all get to bed; and then it began all over again the next morning. Larry was out to sea during this time, and the days were extremely long. Every day I would pray with our children, give them a Mommy-pep talk, and then watch them hold hands as they disappeared behind the walls of those public school doors. How ironic that the school God used me to begin did not include the ages of my own children. Almost every day, after I dropped my children off at their school, I would pull over to the side of the road and have a really good cry for about five minutes while I listened to the Winans sing, "Count it all Joy." After that cleansing cry, I would feel so much better and be ready to greet each student and parent with a smile.

We eventually rented out our home in Hampton in order to move into an apartment in Suffolk, so I could be closer to the school and church. Once we moved to Suffolk, our children could go home right after school, settle down and make friends in their own neighborhood. The school was also able to add more staff and grades that included our son's class, and that was a big relief. Larry was now on shore duty and home more, so eventually we all became better adjusted to our new environment. Nobody has ever said that being obedient to God is easy, because anyone who has heard from Him knows and understands how God will challenge us to do what we think is impossible until we learn that we can do absolutely NOTHING without Him! I asked God, "Why do I have to start this school?" and then, "Why me?" God replied in that soft, gentle voice that pierced my heart and said, "It is not about you." He also reminded me of the times when I had told him during my prayer time that I would do whatever He asked of me, and go wherever he wanted me to go. I do love to travel, and I was quickly learning that an all-knowing God hears us. He wants us to say what we mean and mean what we say to Him, because we will be tested on every word we say and He will reveal wrong or selfish motives to us in order for us to get it right.

A few years later, my family had to leave Suffolk, VA, when my husband received new orders to the USS Kitty Hawk, located in Yokosuka, Japan. I was disappointed that we were leaving during the time shortly after our book was published. I felt that it was selling and doing well. We had already completed several book signings, and most Heaven & Earth book stores in the Hampton Roads area and a few independent stores carried our book. But everything came to a sudden end as the time to promote "*our voices*" had run out as quickly as it had begun due to my departure.

Once I boarded that plane to head across the Atlantic Ocean towards the Pacific, I was so happy in my heart. During that long flight overseas, I talked and prayed to God as I got closer to the ocean I had never seen. I said, "Well God, I did what you told me. I started a Christian school for you, and it is still up and running. Now is my time to work for the government schools and make lots of money overseas where the teachers get paid well and have their own dynamic benefit package." I am sure God was laughing because I was only in Japan for one week before I was approached by a local congregation interested in hiring me to become their principal and launch the first Christian school to ever open up in that city. How they found me was totally a "God-thing," and my plan was to tell the leaders of that church that I would not be available to help with their school. Once again, I was foolish enough to talk with God regarding my own secret agenda. I asked Him to please let Larry give me the final answer to tell the church leaders because my heart was already set on saying, "No." I said to myself (as if God did not see or hear me), "There is no way that man of mine is going to say yes to my beginning another Christian school after all the sacrificing we made as a family with the first school." I went home that day and told Larry at length about the proposal made to me by this particular church. I almost fainted when he exclaimed with glee, "Yes, you have to do this, Dee. Can't you see how this is really what God was preparing you for with the first school back in Virginia?" I fell back into the bedroom wall and slid down to my knees. This time I laughed as I cried, "Uncle" to God. I tore my own agenda into pieces that day and fully accepted my calling.

Japan was also where that young man's second statement became reality for me. He stated that if you change your surroundings, you change who is around you. That statement can be viewed from either an optimistic or pessimistic view. While living in Japan, our surroundings were full of demonic influences and evil powers. We had to fight hard on behalf of our daughter. Our son was at the Christian school with me, but the school did not include our daughter's grade, so she attended school on the base. It was here that our daughter befriended two classmates that neither my husband nor I approved of at all. Our daughter has a very strong will and would sneak out to be around these friends, starting to engage in underage drinking and hanging out way past curfew. Most of the time Larry was out to sea, and I had to be the one to enforce the house rules. Many times our daughter refused to obey, with punishment and discord resulting and continuing in a vicious cycle. My family went through so much more heartache and pain with our daughter than we ever thought possible, while our son adjusted well to Japan.

While it felt like my home would split apart, the Christian school flourished and prospered as God added more children consistently. We had white, black, Japanese, and bi-racial children attending our school, as well as those of non-ranking and high ranking officers as well, and our teaching staff was also multi-racial. The Christian Academy was well on its way to being among the strongest and finest of Christian schools. This was a wonderful achievement, but the problems with our daughter remained, and we eventually had to send her back to the states before the rest of us. The enemy would tell me over and over, "Look at how you failed with your own child while you continued to help other people's children prosper."

Some days those demonic words would discourage my heart. However, it was also in Japan where we were a part of a really strong and supportive ministry. I had an excellent mentor and friend, Co-Pastor Hall, and God was healing some long overdue wounds that should have been dealt with years earlier. I remember one time when I was in a service that our church, Christian Ministries Far East (CMFE), was having, and the power of God was moving mightily. We were at the altar, praying with Asian people who understood our prayers, and many were getting saved, healed, and delivered in miraculous ways. I know it was God who orchestrated our family's move to Japan during that time because Japan is where I discovered the true meaning of the "Balm in Gilead," and I am definitely a much stronger Christian as a result of living and serving in Japan.

Ten years later, our daughter is a high school graduate, the mother of a beautiful little girl, and an LPN. She is currently in school to become an RN. She still has a strong will but is doing well. Our son was an Honor graduate from Potter's House Christian Academy, in Jacksonville, FL, an All-American in football, and is attending college at the University of Mount Union on a football scholarship. The lie satan

(Sue and I refuse to capitalize his name!) attempted to tell me in Japan only builds my testimony today and supports what God spoke into my heart during those difficult moments. "As you take care of my children, I will take care of yours who are really mine." I understand now how all children belong to God. He just loans them to us for a season to train them up properly so they can learn all they can about Him before they enter adulthood. Children have hearts so ripe that all we need to do is plant seeds of righteousness into them, water those seeds with love and encouragement, and God will give the increase. I believe that is why God told me to begin with two-year-olds. They thirst for knowledge better than the middle and high school students I was most experienced with teaching. God continued to remind me that what He had given me to do was not about me at all! I learned as a teacher and a person that truly, "I can do all things through Christ who strengthens me" (Phil. 4:13).

You may recall that I mentioned in an earlier chapter how I did not want to teach or preach - I ran from both of those major assignments. My first responsibilities were to God, my husband and our children, but I began these most important duties as wife and mother with so much fear and insecurity because my childhood experiences and upbringing made me feel inadequate in every area of my life. God helped me discover that home should always come first. In other words, we should not readily desire to minister without (outside our home) until we have found joy and peace from ministering within (our home). It wasn't until I fully accepted the LOVE of Christ into my heart that I could find confidence in fulfilling all of my earthly assignments. The scripture that helped me most is John 3:16, "For God so loved the world that He gave His only begotten Son that whoever believes in Him will not perish, but have everlasting life." (NKJV) Once I fully understood how much God loved me, I could, in turn, love and serve others from that place in God. I know it has absolutely nothing to with me as an individual. The part of ourselves that we share and give to others comes directly from Him in us. As an educator/teacher, I must represent God fully. As an individual person, I must fully represent Him as well. Therefore my vocation, my calling, and my occupation, my career, are so intertwined that I no longer attempt to separate the two. I just live my life as a child of the Most High God.

Maurice Hicks, AKA "Uncle Reece," is a bold Christian who is a nationally and internationally known rapper for Christ. On one of his current CD's he has a song entitled, "Until I Pass Out." The song describes how there is no other option in life but to praise and worship God with all that is in us until we literally pass out from exhaustion. I relate to those lyrics because I love to praise and worship God to the extreme. "Uncle Reese" is also the young man I mentioned throughout this chapter, and I dedicate Ch. XIII to him because so much of what he said to our students that day was so full of truth. While I have never claimed to like any type of rap music, the words to his song and to our students added motivation to my life and totally blessed my soul.

One of the last things "Uncle Reece" said to the students was, "When you focus on the needs of others, your life will be great because living a life full of gratitude to God is what it takes to be successful." What a beautiful way to end this chapter, and all I have to say about that is AMEN!

Sue's Voice:

Wow! After reading Deidre's TYL, all I can say is what a powerful testimony to God's awesome power in turning our insignificant weaknesses into mighty works for Him. Some of her story was familiar to me; other parts I learned for the first time while typing it. No wonder my friend is such a strong Christian—she has been through the trenches and come up a winner through Christ!

Since I have retired not only from my full-time teaching position in Virginia, but now also from my substitute teaching job in our retirement community in West Virginia, I have no new first-hand experiences to relate in my TYL update. I do know teachers who attend my church and a couple of nieces who teach in two different states, so I can tell you that what Deidre and I related in our original publication continues today. Teachers still work day in and day out, dealing with good times and bad. This was brought home to me recently as I joined others to pray for a local middle school which had lost its leader—the principal—to a sudden, unexpected heart attack. So many people of all ages were heartbroken, with the loss of this caring, outgoing, and personable man. The school was rudderless, and to say that teaching, learning, or testing seemed unimportant at this time is definitely an understatement. This is just one example of the challenges inherent in the education profession and in life in general. It can be difficult, even in the best of circumstances to carry on, and when we titled our chapter, *Teachers Are People Too,* we could have just as easily substituted Mechanics, Truck Drivers, or Rappers (Deidre's "Uncle Reece!") for that first word. All of us as adults wear many hats in fulfilling the numerous roles we play in our lives. There never seems to be enough hours in the day to complete everything we need or want to do. Priorities are necessary because some things just have to be removed from the schedule as there is just not enough time for everything.

As Christians and teachers, Deidre and I would emphasize to you that Biblical teaching and church attendance are crucial in raising children today because the world will "beat them down" in many ways. If I as an adult face situations that require a firm hold to my faith and many conversations with God, who is to say that children don't need that foundation as well. How will they learn it if not by being taught from an early age that "Jesus Loves Me . . . This I Know?" My church has several wonderful programs for children as young as two, one of them, Vacation Bible School, which I have directed for several years. What a blessing to enjoy the fruits of my labor by watching children from ages two through twelve sing the songs, do the motions, and recite the Bible verses after only four to five days of fun-filled activities. If little ones can watch and learn to sing, dance, rap, or throw a ball at a young age, they can definitely learn about the God who loves them and will help them through life. It is such a comfort to know you can rely on the One who knew you before you were born to always be there when you need Him.

My faith was tested when our youngest son died, alone, in an apartment in Louisville—hours from home. If I had not had a solid foundation from Bible study, good pastors and Sunday school teachers, and experiences with other strong Christians at my church, I don't know how I would have survived. My peace was God-sent and evident to my family, co-workers, and friends. I was carried through the days, months, and years by my Lord who totally understood what I was experiencing.

The Bible says that God counted my tears as He held me through my grief (Psalm 56:8).

You are a person too, not just the one who waits on customers, fills orders, or drives a taxi. There are times when you need people to understand and appreciate that fact. We all need to consider to whom we are talking when we interact with others during our daily routines. I need reminding from time to time that the driver who just cut me off in traffic may be going through a really hard day and could be dashing to the hospital because a loved one is in trouble. If we all just treated others as we would like to be treated—the Golden, not Silver rule—wouldn't life be so much more enjoyable? That's my encouragement for you today: be someone who makes the world a better place, not one who continues our downward slide. God bless your efforts!

"Do unto others as you would have them do unto you."
—Matthew 7:12

CHAPTER XIV

Just for You —
A God-Shaped Void

"Faith is a gift; but you <u>can</u> ask for it."
—*Fulton Oursler*

Voice II:

I was thinking about this book early one morning when the shower spray was helping me to awaken and shampoo was rinsing down over my forehead. Suddenly, it was as if I received a spiritual message from above, giving me the topic for a concluding chapter. The title, "Just for You—A God-Shaped Void" came to me as I remembered a years-old experience that had faded from my memory. I was walking down the hall of my school when a lovely, young teacher from upstairs came up to me. Out of the blue, she told me that she was searching for meaning in life, and knew I was a Christian. She said that she wanted to know if there was any way I could help her. I remember smiling at her and thinking, "What can I say? God, please don't fail me now!" However, what came out of my mouth was profound and definitely God sent. I told her that the reason she was searching was because her Heavenly Father had created her with a God-shaped void that only He could fill. No matter what she tried instead of Him, she would still be empty and unfulfilled. He was waiting for her to turn to Him. Her face lit up immediately, and she absolutely gushed at me, "That's it—that's perfect! I have been searching everywhere, trying different religions, meditation, yoga—you name it. I always end up feeling worse than ever because nothing ever works." I gave her a hug and later that week brought her a modern translation of the Bible that she and her roommate began reading. At the end of that school year, she moved to a distant state, and I don't know what happened to her or her search. But I do remember the warm, peaceful feeling I experienced as she walked away when I realized that I had been placed in that hall perhaps for the very reason that God needed a messenger to draw a lost child to Him. He gave me that description that so aptly fit her need.

It is only fitting that we end our book with a chapter that gives a new hope and encouragement to those who read it. Since Deidre and I are both Christians and not only draw our strength from each other, but also from our relationship with God, we could not neglect sharing Him with you in a personal way as our book draws to a close. I think God wants you to know just how much He loves you, so He gave me the idea to add this last chapter "just for you."

In my career as a teacher, I have met many people who are in the same situation as that young lady. It's easy to recognize that young people are searching because they have yet to define their identity. However, many adults are just as lost and seem to be looking for meaning to their lives also. No matter how high or low the salary, whether they live in a five-bedroom home or a one-bedroom apartment, drive a BMW or a rusted-out Chevy, adults in this country and around the world are continually searching for the answer to the question, "Why am I here?" An analogy might be the driving, homing instinct that causes salmon to swim against currents, around dams, and incredibly—up waterfalls—as they struggle to reach their ancestral spawning grounds to lay eggs. Humans also have a homing instinct, sixteenth century Protestant theologian, John Calvin, thought when he wrote these words:

"There exists in the human mind, and indeed, by natural instinct, a sense of the Deity."

Augustine, one of the greatest theologians of Western Christianity, speaking of his and other's relationships with God said:

"Hearts are restless until they find their ease (rest) in You."

Current devotional writer, David Roper, continues with the thought:

"We are born and we live for the express purpose of knowing and loving God. He is the source of our life, and our hearts are restless until they come to Him."

Some world religions teach that it takes many levels of consciousness and several lifetimes to perfect life and reach the ultimate goal. Other belief systems tell people to do the best they can for their fellow man, live life to the fullest, and they will be happy. But look into the eyes of the people you see on the street, in the mall, at the gym or the bank, and you will probably see expressions of sadness, desperation, futility, and emptiness. If these people could only learn that their Creator knows and loves them, what a difference that could make in their lives. It is such an awesome thought to realize that the God of the universe is waiting for a one-to-one relationship with each of us. He will not force His way into our lives, but will patiently wait until He is invited.

I would like to encourage each of you to give His Word, the Bible, a chance to explain how you can have the relationship God desires to have with each of you and why it is necessary. In this Book you will find that:

—God loves you and has a great plan for your life. In Genesis 1:27 the Bible says that God created you in His image to have a relationship with Him.

—He wants you to experience a full and wonderful life. In John 10:10, Jesus says that He came to give you "abundant life."

—Something got in the way of our relationship with God. That something is sin. Romans 3:23 says that everyone has "sinned and fallen short of the glory of God." This means that we all have failed to meet God's standard for how we ought to live. We will never live up to His expectations because God is holy and we are not.

—Sin separates us from God and sin always requires punishment. Romans 6:23 states that the "wages of sin is death," which means eternal separation from God. This scripture doesn't leave us hanging there, though, but continues with these words: "but the gift of God is eternal life through Jesus Christ, our Lord."

—God has made a way for us to be forgiven for our sins, and that way was through His Son. Romans 5:8 tells us, "But God demonstrated His love for us in this, that while we were still sinners, Christ died for us."

—God will accept Jesus' death on the cross as payment for our sins.

—Jesus' resurrection from the dead on that first Easter provides our assurance of eternal life through a belief in Him. Jesus himself said in John 14:6 that, "I am the Way, the Truth, and the Life. No one comes to the Father, but through Me."

The choice is up to you. Are you willing to stop living your life without Jesus, turn from your sins, and welcome Him into your heart? Romans 10:9 tells you that:

"If you confess with your mouth 'Jesus is Lord' and believe in your heart that God raised Him from the dead, you will be saved."

Saved from the power of sin! Saved from eternal separation from God in Hell! Saved to live a new life! The Apostle John, the disciple of Jesus said:

"To all who received Him, to those who believed in His name, He gave the right to become children of God."—(John 1:12)

The gift of salvation is just that—a gift from your Heavenly Father (Ephesians 2:8) because if a person could earn it by being good enough, then it wouldn't be free—but it is. How incredibly wonderful is that!

I hope you decide to fill your God-shaped void today with the loving relationship your Heavenly Father wants to give you. Many people will downplay this gospel presentation with a snicker and a laugh, telling you that I am just one of those crazy "right-wing Christians!" However, did they ever stop to think that I just may be right? What if I am? You have everything to gain and nothing to lose by checking out that Book—the Bible. Read it for yourself; maybe starting with the book that the Rev. Billy Graham recommends for new believers— the Gospel of John which you can find in the New Testament. Life today can sometimes be overwhelming. Why go through it alone? Invite Jesus, the Son of God, into your life today and He will be with you now and forever.

Voice I:

In our book's last chapter, I want to conclude with this thought: I believe that one of the greatest errors the Christian community has ever made was to allow God to inadvertently be taken out of our public and some of our private school systems. Like a wobbly house of cards or a line of dominos destined to fall, the effect of this action has led America to begin removing all reference to religion or God in public life. Proof of this can be seen in the current lawsuit to remove the phrase "One Nation Under God" from the Pledge of Allegiance or the actual removal of the Ten Commandments monument from an Alabama courthouse in the summer of 2003. Most recently, I saw a news report about a man who was charged with damaging property in a public library. He destroyed a magazine cover depicting intimate kissing between homosexual men, stating that he felt such a cover was offensive and a detriment to any children who might see it. Instead of choosing to protect its youngest customers, the library is considering legal action against this man, stating that a public library is just that—public—and the magazine should be there for those who want to see and read it.

Many of our forefathers and early settlers who came to this country were God-believing men and women. Their beliefs became the cornerstone and founding principles upon which some of our country's most precious documents were written. The Pilgrims came here for freedom to worship, as did the Quakers who wanted variety in their ways of worship. However, both groups just wished to honor and serve the One, True, Living God. So how is it that a God-based and God-founded country has become so universally accepting and inclusive that we now allow humanistic teachings and ungodly principles to rule in some of our churches and even satanic images to be displayed in some of our schools under the misrepresentation of the first amendment's Freedom of Religion? This amendment gave us the right to worship God as we pleased without the controlling interference of the government. Somehow we have allowed this "separation of church and state" to diminish our voices as Christians and lessen our courage to speak out boldly against these anti-Godly teachings and immoral practices or ideals. Since this country professes to be predominately Christian, the Christian voice should be the one most heard, but it isn't. Every other group tends to influence what we see, hear, and think more than it should. We have shown a lack of unity and example as a God-based nation. It is vital that we return to the truth that God established America, and this young country will not succeed without Him as the basis for how we live our lives.

We are living in a time when abominations unto God are being popularized by television shows and laughed at without any regards to God's Word. The institution of marriage is also becoming a mockery, being damaged beyond repair through the legalization of same-sex unions and the easy availability of divorce because we are not choosing to speak out and protect it. We need to wake up and take America back for God. Phrases like "One Nation Under God," "God Bless America," and "In God We Trust" were not merely statements of chance. They were God-inspired and God-ordained statements of faith given to those men who would begin a proud nation known as these United States of America.

Some of us as Christians are failing to be a prevailing light to a lost and dying world. We are a nation with such a wide divide because we have not put God in His proper place at the head of our lives. We are suffering with a chasm so deep that only God and His Word can fill in the empty spaces. When God created us, he blew a breath of life— a part of Himself—into each of us, so we all share God's DNA, His Spirit. How awesome that all-knowing God could look through the tunnel of time and place a God-shaped desire in each of us in order that mankind could have a relationship and fellowship with Him and be redeemed back to Him. Sin does separate us, but we can be reunited through Jesus Christ. He did this and also gave us the choice to come to Him freely.

Only God can fill the "voids" in our lives because He is the missing piece of the puzzle, the answer to the riddle, and the fulfillment to our individual searches throughout life. We will never be satisfied until we get back to our Father. I am always amazed when adopted children are placed in some of the best homes, yet grow up with an emptiness so prevalent that they feel the need to search for their "real" parents—the source of their origin. Television talk show host, Montel Williams, has often featured segments with siblings and parents being reunited after years of separation. So often these people are able to determine who their true family members are long before it is even revealed. This is because likenesses attract us. It is an instinct of knowing that we belong; there is something in us that recognizes familiarity. Some siblings have the same daddy or the same mom and dad. Likewise, Christians share the same Daddy regardless of race, culture, or denominational differences.

We are all given an opportunity to come back to God, our Creator, and our place of true origin. We can be called the "Sons (Daughters) of God" through the example of our Big Brother, Jesus Christ, whereby we may call out to God, "Abba Father," ("Papa God") and be born again into the Family of God (Galatians 4:3-7 and Romans 8:15 -17). Imagine yourself crawling up into the lap of the One who has all the answers and waits to give you the love you've longed for all your life. He is waiting to supply all your needs and welcome you home. God is our Father—our true Parent. The decision is solely ours. We must choose good over evil, right over wrong, and God's teaching over man's logic and intelligence. The belief in God and His Word is what built America and that is what will sustain us. Righteous living is never easy. When you stand for God's teachings, people sometimes label you a "religious fanatic." Matthew 5:11 quotes Jesus as saying:

"Blessed are you when people insult you, persecute you, and falsely say all kinds of evil against you because of Me."

Matthew 7:13-14 reminds us that it is far easier to go the world's way rather than God's way. It reminds me of a poem Robert Frost concluded with these words:

"I took the road less traveled, and that has made all the difference."

I have come to realize that I have also chosen the less traveled road, God's road. Traveling with Him as He leads has made an important difference in my life which will last into eternity.

TWO VOICES AS ONE...FOR YOU

We would rather stand for God and remain "Small Voices" than to compromise to please man and become well-known ones. The peace that comes from knowing and trusting Him is worth everything. Stop searching for that kind of peace from anything the world may offer. No job, wealth, mate, or goal will ever fulfill what God has already purposed for your life. You can't buy it, but if you seek true meaning for your life, you will find it in God.

"Ask and it will be given to you; seek and you will find; knock and the door will be opened to you. For everyone who asks receives; the one who seeks finds; and to the one who knocks, the door will be opened.—Matthew 7:7-8

"Those who cling to worthless idols forfeit the grace that could be theirs . . . Salvation comes from the Lord."—Jonah 2:8-9

TEN YEARS LATER

Sue's Voice:

In this last TYL update, I think I'm going to go from the "sublime to the ridiculous" to help emphasize my original message to you. The God-shaped void idea that I suggested for Ch. XIV is not unique to me. Since we published our book, I have read several similar sentiments voiced by other authors and speakers, so I have chosen two to speak to you through their bios and words in this final update. The first is Ann B. Davis, who had a long and varied career before audiences ever knew her as Alice on *The Brady Bunch*. This role as a maid to America's favorite blended family made her one of TVs most beloved characters of the day. She played Alice with a deft mix of physical comedy, compassion, and common sense problem-solving. In real life, Davis was a member of the Episcopal School of Ministry, and took classes to study the Anglican tradition. In an interview with *People* magazine in 1992, she talked about the religion that meant so much to her with these words:

> "My mother would write letters when I was away at camp and say, 'There's an Ann-shaped space around the house. Nobody fills an Ann-shaped space except an Ann. I'm convinced we all have a God-shaped space in us, and until we fill that space with God, we'll never know what it is to be whole."

Describing herself as "born again," her caring nature showed through her role, and viewers "didn't have to be related to relate to her" as one

TV critic put it. Everyone loved Alice - the Dear Abby, Julia Child, and Lucille Ball character all rolled into one.

That's my sublime example of someone who understood and quoted my idea of an inborn need and space that only God can fill so well. Are you ready for the ridiculous illustration? Here he comes!

Born Vincent Damon Furnier, this musician shot to stardom in the 1970s/80s with such hits as "I'm 18" and "Schools Out." Notorious for his demonic makeup, costumes, and macabre theatrics on state, he was definitely a "dark" performer. Nominated for two Grammy awards, he and his band were inducted into the Rock and Roll Hall of Fame in 2011. You know him as Alice Cooper, but I'll bet you don't know that he and his wife were both PKs (preacher's kids). To quote Cooper from an interview he posted on YouTube, "I grew up in a Christian house. My dad was a pastor and evangelist for 25 years. My grandfather was a pastor for 75 years and my wife's father is a Baptist pastor. I always refer to myself as the real Prodigal Son because the Lord let me do everything," said Cooper. "Maybe didn't let me but allowed it, and then just started reeling me back in . . . you know, you've seen enough. Let's bring you back to where you belong. When you get out there and realize you've had every car, every house, and all that, you realize that that's not the answer. There's a big nothing out there at the end of all that. So materialism doesn't mean anything. A lot of people say that there's a big God-sized hole in your heart, and when that's filled, you're really satisfied. That's where I am right now." Continuing, Cooper says his early songs always warned against choosing evil and picking the devil's way. He contends that the world we live in "doesn't belong to us, it belongs to Satan. We're living with that—bombarded with that every day."

The shock-rock megastar stopped his partying ways, quit drinking alcohol, and started going back to church, returning to his Bible Christian roots in the late 1980s. "I realized that I had to go to one way or the other; I had to make a decision, and my life has changed for the better."

Well, there you go—if you won't listen to me or to the Brady's Alice, maybe you'll respond to this other Alice. He definitely experienced both sides of life before he came to realize that Jesus Christ has the answers. One final quote of his really struck me when he said the following to his fans, those who are still following the 'sex, drugs, and rock-and-roll' lifestyle and not following Jesus: "Well, they're going to eventually know Christ, and I hope it's not too late. If you're at the wrong end at the wrong time, I think that's going to be tragic."

Deidre and I began this book as two teachers writing to describe our daily experiences and support the education profession. Somehow, it turned into more of an evangelical progression through the ins and outs of everyone's daily life and the struggles most of us face. I'm not surprised, since a lot of Christians realize that we are going through "warfare" every day as the world turns in the wrong direction. I hope we have encouraged you to take the right path, trust God and His Word when making decisions, and follow the greatest commandment to "love God with all your heart, soul, and mind, and love your neighbor as yourself" (Matt. 22:37-39). It's the only way to survive with your head looking up, awaiting His return. Thank you for considering our "voices." We would love to hear from you and share yours as well.

God bless you!

Deidre's Voice:

I wanted Sue's voice to go first again on these TYL chapters because of the people she used to further illustrate and expound on her God-shaped void message from ten years ago. Most of us realize that there is nothing new under the sun because that is a truth spoken of in the Bible. There are, however, so many ways of saying the same or very similar things as Sue so practically demonstrated in her TYL of this chapter. Sue's use of Alice Cooper is simply a profound example. His comments on how he made a decision to leave one side and go to the other side was really about his personal choices. Cooper further stated how returning to God turned out to be the best decision he had ever made. In other words, he chose God, and that is exactly what we all have to do.

Salvation is a choice, as is serving and living for God. The Bible tells us in John 15:16 NIV that God made a choice of us, "You did not choose me, but I chose you and appointed you so that you might go and bear fruit." Once He chose us, we then had a choice in how we responded. We can choose to ignore God's choice of us, or we can choose to hear, receive, and follow Him for life. I tell students all the time that life is full of choices. Every day we make hundreds of choices from the time we get out of bed in the morning until the time we return to bed at night. We choose the thoughts that begin our day, so I tell students to practice this simple but essential habit: "Wake up and Look up! Look up to your Creator and begin each day with telling Him thanks for allowing you to wake up to a new day and follow that by asking God for direction for that one new day (Proverbs 3:5-8)."

Furthermore, we must love and accept and choose the one true God, Jesus Christ, as the God we will serve. Joshua boldly declared to his people, "But if serving the Lord seems undesirable to you, then **choose for yourselves** this day whom you will serve, whether the gods your ancestors served beyond the Euphrates or the gods of the Amorites, in whose land you are now living. But as for me and my household, we will serve the Lord!" (Joshua 24:15 NIV) Still, Jesus said it best in Luke 9:23 NIV, "Then He said to them all, if anyone desires to come after Me, let him deny himself, and take up his cross daily and follow me."

In this day and age, we have so much information about God, the Bible, salvation, and any other theological topic known to man. One tap of the finger tip can open up all kinds of material and information that at one time would take hours, days, or even years of research. Now we can access it within minutes. Even if you cannot read or do not like to read, someone else will read to you via e-books, cell phone, or the internet. We are without excuse.

Therefore, we have to choose to fill our lives with God daily. Four or five hours of TV, golf, the beach, a basketball game, video games, or the internet can go by so quickly without any complaints, but we have a serious problem with an hour sermon or a two-three hour church service. We may also choose to focus on ourselves and only what matters to us each day. We may never choose to offer our service or our gifts and talents to God's kingdom or others in need. However, many people choose to offer their services to the evil one as Alice Cooper did for years before deciding to give back to God what belongs to Him anyway—himself! Once God has made known to us His choice of us, we have to respond with a proper choice. We must choose today, "yes" to salvation and "yes" to our call and purpose. Then we must consistently choose Him over the house, the car, the hobby, the favorite sport, the special vacation spot, or that special person. Of course God wants us to enjoy our lives with people, places, and things, but none of those things should be our focus or idol because the spiritual part of our beings is actually who we really are.

When we lose our spouse, a parent, a child, our home, or any other grand possession, we cannot stop living our lives or lose our minds. Sue knows and understands this first-hand. She has lost both of her parents and a child, but she continues to live her life and continues to serve and choose God in spite of those awful circumstances. We must all choose to live life to the fullest by choosing God and His ways. Who Christ was, is, and will continue to be for us and the life we allow Him to live inside of us is the only way we can truly and completely fill that God-shaped void.

ABOUT THE AUTHORS

Voice I:

Deidre Boone Hester is a published author, educator, counselor, and minister of the Gospel. She and her husband, Larry, were both ministers with True Gospel Ministries Evangelical House of God, in Suffolk, VA at the time of the **Small Voices** book's first publication. They have been married for 26 of their 34 years of close friendship. They have two grown children, Shamona and Larry, Jr., and also boast of one beautiful granddaughter, seven-year-old, Saniyah Grace. The family resides in Jacksonville, Florida, where they attend and serve at The Potter's House International Ministries.

Voice II:

Sue E. Whited and her husband, Richard, were both teachers with Hampton City Schools in Hampton, VA, when the original book was published in 2004. Mrs. Whited graduated from Christopher Newport College (now University) in Newport News, VA, and taught sixth and eighth grade students the subjects of reading and social studies for almost twenty years. Retiring in June 2005, they moved to their home state of WV, building their retire-ment home in the "Whited Woods" of Washington, WV. Sue and her husband are the parents of two sons, Ric and Bryan (deceased), and attend Fairlawn Baptist Church in Parkersburg, WV, where she is active in the music ministry, food pantry, and also directs the church's Vacation Bible School. Using their free time to travel and camp has been very enjoyable, as are frequent trips back to Virginia to visit family and friends.

THE TWO VOICES: THEN AND NOW

THEN   NOW

A FOREVER FRIEND IS A GIFT FROM GOD

ACKNOWLEDGEMENTS

We dedicate this book in honor of our Lord and Savior, Jesus Christ, to Whom it all belongs. "Thank you, Lord, for giving us the grace to continue our book ministry. It is all done to your glory, and the results still belong to you."

Voice I:

I wish to give special thanks to:

Sue Edwards, for her prayers, support, and hard work as our friend and personal editor.

Sue and Richard Whited, for being our mentors for life and our most devoted friends; specifically to Richard for your labor of love on the book cover, then and now.

My husband, Larry, for covering me fully, for his unconditional love, prayers, undying support, hard work for our family, and laughter when I needed it the most.

My children, Larry and Shamona, and our granddaughter, Saniyah, for sharing your mother's/grandmother's time, love, and hugs with so many others, unselfishly.

My faithful prayer partners and friends from True Gospel Ministries (TGM), Christian Ministries Far East (CMFE), The Potter's House International Ministries (TPHIM), Livingstone College, and my other family members (Boone/Hester) for all of your love, support, and encouraging words throughout the many stages of my life.

My pastor and first lady, Bishop Vaughn and Lady Narlene McLaughlin, for loving and supporting me and my family unconditionally. Thank you, Lady, for being there with counseling and encouragement from the beginning until now, and to Bishop Vaughn for that awesome teaching and SURE WORD.

Bishop Daniel and Lady Boone for allowing God to use you to bring salvation to the Boone family and to help deliver so many of us from those inevitable generational curses. You truly taught me about holiness.

Bishop and Co-Pastor Hall for loving us, teaching and helping us to grow up fast in the work of the ministry by using and sharpening our gifts; for placing your trust in me to lead and share a part of history by the Christian Achievement Academy (CAA) becoming the first Christian school in Yokosuka, Japan. Thank you, Co-Pastor Hall for showing me through God's Word my value as a woman, a mother, and a minister; also, for being willing and accessible to help mentor me as I mentor others.

All the others who may not fit in one of the above mentioned categories: friends, students, parents, former colleagues and other loved ones. I wish to acknowledge you also for being in my life for the reason God intended. Thank you, everyone!

Voice II:

During this rewrite process, I was reminded how much this book depended on the involvement of others:

First of all is my gratitude to Deidre, my lifeline and friend, who has impacted my life in so many positive ways. God put our lives together for many reasons—friendship, encouragement, fun, and, I believe, to impact the lives of others. This book is one of the ways we hope to do that.

Secondly, I continue to realize how important my upbringing was in molding me into the person I am, and for that I want to thank my parents, A. Paul Saunders and Gretta Stewart Saunders. I could always count on their prayers and support and I am indeed thankful that I grew up in a home where God was a part of my life for as long as I can remember.

Next, I want to give a loving "thank you" to my husband, Richard, for all his help with our cover design and the many computer changes, and his playful encouragement for both Deidre and me. Don't ask what his choice was for our title!

I want to extend my appreciation to my oldest son, Ric, who taught me how to be a Mom and a teacher throughout his life, and helped me learn about unconditional love as well.

I will always be grateful that Sue Edwards was placed into my life. My endless thanks to her—administrator "extraordinaire," teacher, colleague, and friend—for many reasons, but especially for proofing our book and encouraging our efforts.

I want to again thank Dr. Daniel Forshee for his ministerial help and insight in helping to proof Ch. XIV for our original publication. He was my pastor at the time we wrote our **Small Voices** book, and is blessing another congregation now in Austin, Texas.

I am so appreciative for the work of our publisher, David L. Hancock, of Morgan James Publishing for his willingness to work with us on our timetable. Always pleasant and encouraging, David has consistently been a Godsend.

Since we dedicated this book to God, we want to thank Him for bringing the "voices" together in the first place. We had no idea what our friendship would mean to us or others, but we have learned to trust Him and follow where He leads.

Printed in the USA
CPSIA information can be obtained
at www.ICGtesting.com
JSHW082229140824
68134JS00017B/804